PERSONALITY AND POLITICS

PERSONALITY AND POLITICS

Obama For and Against Himself

Stephen J. Wayne
Georgetown University

CQ PRESS

A Division of SAGE
Washington, D.C.

CQ Press
2300 N Street, NW, Suite 800
Washington, DC 20037

Phone: 202-729-1900; toll-free, 1-866-4CQ-PRESS (1-866-427-7737)

Web: www.cqpress.com

Cover design: Anne C. Kerns, Anne Likes Red, Inc.
Cover photo: AP Photo/Haraz N. Ghanbari
Composition: C&M Digitals (P) Ltd.

♾ The paper used in this publication exceeds the requirements of the American
National Standard for Information Sciences—Permanence of Paper for Printed
Library Materials, ANSI Z39.48-1992.

Printed and bound in the United States of America

15   14   13   12   11   1   2   3   4   5

Library of Congress Cataloging-in-Publication Data

Wayne, Stephen J.
   Personality and politics : Obama for and against himself / Stephen J. Wayne.
      p. cm.
   Includes bibliographical references and index.
   ISBN 978-1-60871-694-4 (pbk. : alk. paper) 1. Obama, Barack. 2. Obama,
Barack—Psychology. 3. United States—Politics and government—2009- 4. United
States—Politics and government—2009—Psychological aspects. I. Title.

   E908.W39 2012
   973.932092—dc22

                                                                2010052878

Dedicated to Cheryl with Love

CONTENTS

BOXES, FIGURES, AND TABLES

PREFACE

Presidents have mystiques. They are created by their achievements; enhanced and projected by their campaigns; and enlarged by the status, responsibilities, and powers of their office. At times presidents appear to be larger than life, depending on the perception, sometimes awe-inspiring and sometimes terrifying, sometimes inspirational and sometimes mundane, sometimes strong and other times weak, even infirm.

The office of the presidency envelops the person in it. It can highlight strengths of character, but it can also magnify personal frailties. At times it may be difficult to discern the person from the office; the human dimension is often obscured by the institutional protections and majestic qualities Americans desire and perceive in their presidents.

Much of the political science literature focuses on the institutional influences on presidents: the roles they are expected to perform, the authority they have to exercise, the political clout they can exert, the decisions they must make, the relations they have with others in positions of power, and the images they try to project of themselves and their administrations.

But presidents influence the presidency as well by the words they use, the roles they emphasize, the decisions they make, the actions they take, all of which in turn are affected by what they believe and how they go about their work.

This book focuses on that human dimension of the presidency. It examines how President Barack Obama's character, beliefs, and operating style have affected the first two years of his presidency. Obviously, personal attributes cannot be examined in isolation. They must be viewed within the context of the constitutional, institutional, and political systems as well as the events and environment with which presidents have to contend. Much of my discussion occurs within this framework.

My objective is to paint a character portrait of the man and use that portrait to help explain his decisions and actions as president. I do not contend that everything Obama says or does is driven by his personality, but I do believe that personality matters and has an impact on many of the most important decisions presidents make and actions they take.

I begin my study by looking at character development: how Obama sees himself. He eloquently (and with considerable literary license) wrote about his identity search in his book, *Dreams from My Father*. I am interested in what he found in that search that has enabled him to understand who he is, what he desires, enjoys, and excels in doing, and how that understanding has shaped his personal quest, political ambitions, and ultimately, his actions as president.

I argue that Obama's values and beliefs are a product of his identity search, the opportunities he has had to pursue a career in law and public service, and the people he has encountered who have helped him to achieve personal and social goals. I am most interested in his beliefs about government that have shaped his political vision and policy positions as candidate and then as president.

I also believe that presidential style, the way in which a president goes about the work of the office, has an impact on that president's decisions and actions. In Obama's case, I believe that his style is distinguishable by how he interacts with three sets of people: those whose support he needs to gain elective office, those whose analyses and advice he relies on to make sound policy judgments, and those whose approval and friendship he craves for any number of personal reasons.

The relative stability of character, beliefs, and style results in patterned behavior. That behavior, in turn, facilitates the psychological dimension of explanation, and to some extent, anticipated behavior. I examine these behavioral patterns throughout this book.

Nonetheless, there can also be character-based inconsistencies that create tensions for an individual. I discuss some of these tensions that have affected Obama in the presidency as well as the major political challenges he has encountered, challenges to which his 2008 presidential campaign contributed. I also examine Obama's theory of participatory democracy and his actions as president that seem to conflict with that theory. My objective throughout is to provide a critical but not hostile evaluation of the Obama presidency, one that uses the prisms of personality and politics to explain President Obama's performance in office.

Acknowledgments

I wish to thank the many people who have helped me with this project.

- The reviewers of my initial book proposal to CQ Press: Holly Brasher (University of Alabama), Fred I. Greenstein (Princeton University), and Lauri McNown (University of Colorado).
- Colleagues who have read and critiqued presentations and papers that evolved into this manuscript: Thomas E. Cronin (Colorado College), Fred I. Greenstein (Princeton University), James Pfiffner (George Mason University), and Stanley Renshon (CUNY-Graduate Center).
- The editorial and production staff at CQ Press: Charisse Kiino, editorial director; Debbie Hardin, freelance copyeditor; and Belinda Josey, production editor.

Most of all, I want to thank my wife, Dr. Cheryl Beil, for her unrelenting encouragement and support as well as for relieving me of my family responsibilities so I could work alone during the summer of 2010 at our retreat in Vermont. It was Cheryl's work in social psychology, and particularly her practice of our family psychology through the years, that has fueled my interest in the personality dimension of presidential leadership. It is to Cheryl with love and gratitude that I dedicate this book.

PERSONALITY AND POLITICS

PRESIDENTIAL CHARACTER: AN INTRODUCTION

It matters who is president. Why else have elections? The mindset that presidents bring to their tasks—their basic assumptions, opinions, and beliefs—the thought processes they use to reach decisions, the reactions they have to unanticipated situations, the emotions they display about particular issues, people, and events, and even their willingness to revisit decisions and actions once made have a unique dimension to them, which is shaped in part by their personalities. Character affects what presidents say and do and how they relate to others. It is a dimension of any behavioral explanation.

Why would a well-informed, intelligent, and skillful man, such as Woodrow Wilson—president of Princeton, governor of New Jersey, and president of the United States—become so rigid in the face of opposition to the Versailles Treaty and the League of Nations at the end of his second term in office? Why would a long-time, national public figure, who served in the House, Senate, and as vice president, Richard Nixon, take tax write-offs that he did not need and cover up a burglary that he did not order? Why would an experienced politician, such as Lyndon Johnson, who, as president, achieved the most comprehensive economic and social reforms since the New Deal get so deeply and hopelessly mired in a war in Southeast Asia? Why would Jimmy Carter, whose innovative campaign and down-to-earth style propelled him into the White House, have such difficulty dealing with the Washington political establishment, especially with members of Congress and the news media? In contrast, why would Ronald Reagan, a movie actor with no national governing experience and strong ideological views, interact so easily and effectively with that Washington community? Why would an experienced politician, George H. W. Bush,

Reagan's vice president for eight years, a man who had come from behind to win the general election in 1988, not emphasize the public dimensions of his office, fail to stick to his campaign promise not to raise taxes, and do so little to plan for his reelection campaign? Why would Bill Clinton, an ambitious person who wanted to be president since high school, avoid the draft, smoke pot, and engage in multiple sexual encounters before he ran for the presidency? Why would George W. Bush, who idolized his father and was heir to the Bush family legacy, also engage in what could be interpreted as dysfunctional behavior in his first forty years? And why would Barack Obama, who inspired so many people with his campaign oratory and his promises to change policy and politics in Washington evoke the emotions of so many angry people during his first two years as president?

An analysis of presidential character can help answer these questions and help explain what politics may not be able to do alone—why presidents at times say and do seemingly irrational and unexpected things, and why candidates who show so much promise as campaigners have such difficulty governing and others who barely won govern so successfully.

Newly elected presidents do not leave their personalities on the doorstep when they enter the Oval Office. They are still basically the same people they were before being elected, but in the office of president they have many more responsibilities and much more power. The impact of their decisions and actions from ordering military actions to regulating business activities to setting environmental standards, safeguarding national security, and even promoting democratic beliefs and values in the United States and abroad, can be enormous. Moreover, the American people see them more clearly, closely, and critically than they do any other public official. That is why it is important to examine the character of presidential candidates and equally important to assess their character as president.

Character is relatively stable. Once developed, it changes slowly. Personal behavior tends to be repetitive over time. If patterns of words and actions can be identified, they can help explain and to some extent even predict reactions. Thus, knowing a president's character provides a guide to understanding and anticipating their words and actions as president.

Character is not good or bad per se. It is the fit between the person, the institution, and the environment that matters most. On the job learning is also important. Presidents need to be able to adjust to unexpected events and changing conditions. They need to have the skills to exercise power but also to appreciate its dangers and limits. For all these reasons, it is important to examine the influence of a president's character on performance in office.

Unfortunately, the study of character is one of the least analyzed aspects of presidential behavior. The institution of the presidency, its evolution and operation, its interaction with the other two branches of government, the scope and exercise of its constitutional and statutory authority, the president's political influence and rhetorical skills, have received considerably more scholarly attention than has the relationship between character and performance. Why?

The short answer is that the goals of contemporary political science and the methods currently in vogue to examine political behavior are not easily amenable to the study of an individual president's character and its influence on how that president thinks, speaks, decides, and behaves in office. The next section briefly explains the dilemma political scientists face when studying presidential character.

A Disciplinary Dilemma

Why do political scientists find the study of presidential character and its impact so difficult? One reason stems from the kinds of decisions presidents make and the actions they take. The situations in which personality factors are likely to have a greater influence tend to be the ones that are most important and controversial, not those that are simple, routine, or easily delegable. Such decisions also tend to be the most complex, with many variables potentially affecting the outcome, variables such as past performance, precedent, partisanship, politics, institutional processes, internal group dynamics, and public expectations. Add to these, the perceptions, assumptions, thinking, and emotions of the president and others involved in presidential decisions and actions, the urgency of the matter, and the time frame in which it occurs, and the list of potential contributing factors becomes larger and larger. Identifying all of them is hard enough, but assessing their impact individually and collectively is even harder.

Complexity is not the only problem for political scientists. Character is not directly observable. It is inferred from behavior on the basis of theories proposed by psychiatrists and psychologists.[1] Political scientists do not like to make such inferences. They prefer to identify and measure data that they can observe directly.

A third issue that complicates the study of character is the difficulty of generalizing from a single or small number of cases. Not only are people unique, but the situations in which presidents find themselves may be unique as well. The idiosyncratic aspects of a president's decision or action, set within the context of the situation, cloud underlying commonalities that detract from the generalizability of the findings.

To achieve the goals of hypothesis testing and theory building, most political scientists eliminate what they consider to be extraneous detail. They simplify in order to generalize. Simplification reduces the external validity of the research. It creates a potential reality gap between the model used to explain the behavior and the actual situation in which that behavior occurs. Models simplify to clarify, but in the process they do not convey the complexity that characterizes real world experiences.

Other problems stem from the vantage point of the researcher and the methods of analysis. Scholars taking a presidential-centered approach—looking over the president's shoulder, as it were, such as Richard E. Neustadt did in his well-known book, *Presidential Power*[2]—see a larger and more visible presidential hand exercising influence than do scholars who try to measure that influence from a distance by studying factors that may be a product of that influence, such as roll call votes in Congress or public approval of the president's job performance. Researchers who have applied quantitative methodologies to study congressional voting behavior or public opinion have not discovered much evidence of discernible presidential influence.[3] The old adage, "where you stand affects what you see," is applicable here.

The qualitative or quantitative nature of the study also affects the scope and content of the findings. Qualitative studies can capture rich detail and improve external validity, but they do not facilitate precise measurement or permit behavioral comparisons from which generalizations can be made. Quantitative analyses, on the other hand, sacrifice richness for simplicity to identify, measure, and test relationships from which researchers can generalize.

Each perspective and methodology involves trade-offs that scholars make when they design their research and perform their analyses. The goal of their research shapes their findings. The current emphasis on postulating theories that contain testable hypotheses has discouraged many political scientists from studying how the personality dimensions of individual presidents influence their performance in office.

However, ignoring the influence that a president's character may have on judgment and actions because it is difficult to study scientifically flies in the face of conventional wisdom that people can and do affect the decisions they make and the actions they take. It also ignores a body of psychological literature that contains theories of personality derived from clinical observation, experimental design, psychometric measurement, social interaction, organizational leadership, and environmental influences on individual and group behavior.[4] Finally, it neglects a newer area of research in which genetic components of attitude formulation and political activity are being identified and measured.[5]

There is no magic formula to understanding the president in the presidency. In this study, my vantage point is Barack Obama. My objective is to explain his presidency on the basis of what he personally brought to the office, how he has confronted his duties and responsibilities, and what he has learned thus far as president.

To achieve my objective, I first describe Obama, the person—what makes him tick. Character development is important in the behavior of a president. It conditions beliefs and operating style. There is not a perfect character type for the presidency.[6] Any personal trait can have a positive or negative effect, depending on the circumstances. However, circumstances change while personalities are relatively constant. Thus, it is important to explore the interaction of personal and situational factors to determine when and how the attributes of a person—in this case President Obama—work to his advantage or disadvantage.

Character and Its Derivatives

In his book, *The Presidential Character,* James David Barber defines *character* as a basic orientation toward life, how people view themselves.[7] For Barber, character is developed from personal experience. That experience affects cognition, beliefs, decision making, communication, and social relationships.

Stanley Renshon, a psychoanalyst and political scientist, describes character as "the basic foundation upon which personality structures develop and operate."[8] He argues that character shapes how information is processed, decisions are made and executed, and behavioral patterns established. For Renshon, the dimensions of character that most directly affect political activity are *ambition, integrity, and relatedness.*[9]

Ambition provides the motivation to pursue and achieve political goals. Without motivation, people would be unlikely to undergo the rigors of campaigning and governing, endure the criticism that occurs within both venues, and suffer the loss of privacy that a public career entails today.

Although ambition is necessary, too much of it can be dangerous. It can warp perceptions; obscure reality; interfere with good judgment; and lead to rigidity in thinking, deciding, and acting. Overly ambitious people may stop at nothing to succeed. Nixon and Clinton are examples of contemporary presidents whose uncontrolled personal ambition marred their professional judgments and credibility. Nixon sought to cover up the involvement of the White House in the Watergate burglary; Clinton lied about an extramarital affair he had with a White House intern that began in his first term for fear that if he admitted it, he would not be reelected. Both lacked sufficient emotional intelligence, according to presidential scholar Fred I. Greenstein. Greenstein maintains that they let their personal needs and anxieties affect their political and policy decisions.[10]

Integrity is the capacity to remain true to one's ideals, values, and beliefs. Integrity provides an ethical framework for understanding and making judgments within a larger social context. Politicians who lack integrity tend to be driven by their own self-interests, which they often rationalize in terms of the public good. Acting in accordance with one's beliefs and values, which are usually articulated in an electoral campaign, is meritorious and consistent with responsive government.

The danger comes when conditions change, when new issues arise, the public mood shifts, but elected officials continue to pursue their old policies and the beliefs that underlie them, as if nothing had changed. George W. Bush faced such a situation after his reelection in 2004. After public support for the Iraq War declined sharply, the president did not change his policy objectives. As a consequence, his job approval suffered.

On the other hand, frequent position shifts to conform to the mood of the moment may also be undesirable for the president and unnerving for the public. Changes in priorities, issue positions, and even observable behavior raise questions about a president's credibility, reliability, and judgment. Such changes can undermine a leadership image. Take John McCain's actions during his 2008 campaign. He accused Obama of lacking governing experience at the national level and then chose a running mate who had even less national governing experience. As the financial markets were collapsing in mid-September 2008, McCain said, "Our economy, I think, still the fundamentals of our economy are strong."[11] A few days later he suspended his campaign to return to Washington to participate in White House–congressional deliberations on the economic downturn, the solvency of large investment and insurance firms, and the government's response to the rapidly worsening situation in the United States. According to *Newsweek* reporter Jonathan Alter, McCain contributed little to these discussions.[12] McCain's actions appeared to be inconsistent and erratic, terms that the Obama campaign used frequently to bring attention to McCain's behavior during a crisis.[13]

Renshon argues that both ambition and integrity are necessary and desirable attributes for a public official such as a president. He states that ambition in the pursuit of ideals contributes to a strong sense of self, but warns that ambition in the pursuit of self-interest does not.[14]

Relatedness concerns interactions with others. Interactions can be friendly or hostile, intimate or distant, spontaneous or contrived. Obviously, elective politicians must relate to a diverse public. Clinton was particularly effective in social relations, which supporters attributed to his out-going personality and natural political skills but opponents saw as manipulative and deceptive. George W. Bush got along well with small groups of "regular folks," especially those who had political dispositions and beliefs similar to his; Bush did less well in situations in which inquisitiveness, incisiveness, sophisticated discussion, and educated explanations were expected. In his book, *The Audacity of Hope,* Obama described Bush as likeable, shrewd, and disciplined, "the kind of guy who would make for good company so long as the conversation revolved around sports and kids."[15]

The personal experience that shapes character also conditions beliefs, ways of thinking, and styles of behaving. Beliefs, which are formulated as people become aware of the world around them and seek to understand it, are guides to judgment. They help frame the mindset that presidents bring to the Oval Office; they affect how presidents perceive reality, what information they regard as important, and how they process that information. Character also has something to do with a president's proclivity for sticking to his judgments once made or changing them in light of public disapproval, new evidence, or changing conditions.

Presidential candidates go to great lengths to articulate their beliefs and the belief systems that tie those beliefs together. In doing so, they create expectations that they will act in a certain way. If they do not do so, their credibility will be undermined. From a public perspective, steadiness in decision making is more often a virtue than a liability.

Ronald Reagan and George W. Bush were guided by their conservative views throughout their presidencies. Clinton and Obama were less ideological and more pragmatic; their actions as president were also less predictable and more equivocal than their Republican predecessors.

Style, another derivative of character, is the *way* we go about doing things. Style conditions social interactions and personal and public communications. It is patterned behavior. People adopt styles to project their most desirable traits and hide their least desirable ones. Style is thus an instrument for protecting and enhancing self-image.

According to Barber, political style is developed at the time of a person's first political success.[16] The style works to achieve particular, personal goals and will be used again and again until it no longer works. When a particular style impedes rather than facilitates the desired end, it's time to make adjustments or face failure. In the first year of his presidency, Obama delegated much of the design and implementation of his major policy goals to Congress. That delegation dragged out the policy-making process and undermined the leadership image Obama projected during his presidential campaign. During the health care debate, Obama was forced to take a more assertive leadership role to be successful. To appear to be in charge, he had to take charge.

George W. Bush faced a similar perceptual issue when he entered the presidency. His 2000 campaign, which was short on policy specifics, created an impression that he would be overly dependent on others, most notably Vice President Dick Cheney. The White House attempted to counter this impression during the president's first months in office by having Bush deliver policy-specific speeches across the country, keeping Cheney out of the public view, and leaking to the news media that every major decision was made by the president.

The terrorist attacks of September 11, 2001, allowed Bush to redefine his presidency and recast his leadership image. However, once Bush redefined his role as a war-time president, the person in charge, he could not escape criticism when his decisions and actions in the war on terrorism and other government actions or inactions, such as the response to Hurricane Katrina, were called into question. The challenge for presidents is to be themselves, demonstrate the personal qualities that helped get them elected, and at the same time be sufficiently flexible to learn on the job. If presidents find that their beliefs need to be modified and their operating style adjusted, they must do so in a way that does not undermine their authenticity, credibility, and strength of character.

Presidential advisers in the realm of public relations sometimes try to change a president's image. For example, Nixon developed an image of being a no-holds-barred politician in his early years campaigning for office. His advisers tried to soften that image and present him as a statesman, but they were unable to change Nixon's personality, which showed through the veneer his public relations experts had designed. Because changing one's basic character is so difficult (if not impossible), such image crafting generally fails. The bottom line is that character and its derivatives, beliefs, and behavior are stable. They are the product of years of development. They are a compilation of life's experiences—and all of this is difficult to undo.

Organization of the Book

Presidents do not (and cannot) discard their personalities when they enter the White House. Traits that they exhibited in the past affect their current and future behavior. The inescapability of these effects are precisely why the study of presidential character and its derivatives, beliefs, and operating style, are so important—and they are my principal focus in this book.

Chapter 1 examines Obama's basic character. It begins with a discussion of his search for identity; what he found; how it shaped his needs, hopes, and dreams; and how he applied it in the pursuit of his political ambitions as well as his personal quest to find purpose, satisfaction, and happiness. The chapter also discusses Obama's adaptive skills and how they have helped him gain acceptance, approval, and achievement. Finally, the ego checks Obama imposes on himself and the guilt he has felt for his nonstop political career are noted.

Chapter 2 explores Obama's beliefs and the assumptions on which they are based. Here I examine the nexus between character and world view—how Obama's beliefs resulted from his search for roots, his desire to bridge the multiple divides that separate Americans, and his understanding of the uniqueness of the American experience, the country's success in integrating so many diverse cultures into a single union. In this chapter, I also discuss Obama's views of community and its importance, his perspective on organized religion and spiritualism, and the part they have played in his adult life. I then turn to Obama's beliefs about government, the roles he believes he should perform as president, and the tension it creates when government becomes a force for social and economic change.

How Obama has negotiated that tension on a group and personal level leads into Chapter 3. Here I look at Obama's operating style, how he thinks, decides, communicates, and manages himself and those around him. His style is a product of his experience as an organizer, lawyer, and politician; a candidate, legislator, and president; a citizen, representative, and political and social leader. It is consistent with his need to accommodate others and find common ground, two values that he holds strongly. Finally, Chapter 3 discusses Obama's temperament, which he considers to be an important component of his leadership style and one of the reasons why he won the election.

Chapter 4 turns to character-based contradictions and tensions: Obama's lofty ideals and pragmatic outlook, his leadership aspirations and propensity to delegate, his judgmental confidence and willingness to compromise, his boldness, vision, and risk-averse decisions, and his rational manner and the problems it presents for reaching out and showing empathy.

Chapter 5 turns from stylistic tensions to political ones. It discusses why Obama's promise to change "politics as usual" in Washington has failed thus far. In this chapter, I turn first to the transition from campaigning to governing, noting the differences between these two functions and explaining the problems of moving from candidate to president. I then discuss the limits on presidential power, a constitutional system that separates institutions and shares powers, a federalized party structure that has become highly polarized along ideological lines, and the institutional and personal rivalries that characterize contemporary American politics. I also look at the tension between a president who desires an activist government and a public skeptical and mistrustful of such a government, particularly the exercise of strong, centralized authority in the economic and domestic realms.

In Chapter 6, I explore another dilemma that Obama has faced as president: the leader-follower paradox within a democratic society. An advocate of participatory democracy in his writings and campaign oratory, Obama has had to contend with a public divided in its opinions and angry or apathetic much of the time. In this chapter I discuss how the president reconciles his roles as steward and delegate of the people, teacher and student, advocate and responsive policy maker. I examine the pros and cons of going public. I also discuss Obama's exercise of democratic leadership. The chapter poses a quandary: Can Obama exercise the democratic leadership he postulated during his campaign, replete with public debate, participatory democracy, bipartisanship, and common ground solutions, or has the environment in which he must operate forced him to be a partisan, Democratic leader?

Chapter 7 looks at the impact of personality and politics on three of the president's major policy decisions: his proposal to stimulate the economy, expand American military involvement in Afghanistan, and pursue health care reform after the Democrats' electoral defeats in 2009 and January 2010 and growing public opposition to the legislation. In each of these cases, I look at Obama's advising system, decision-making process, and policy judgments within the context of stylistic traits and political environment discussed in previous chapters.

My analysis is inevitably subjective based on my knowledge and interpretation of Obama's words and actions. The data I rely on for this study come primarily from Obama's two books and literally hundreds of interviews he has had during his political career. In addition, I have examined speeches in which he has played a large role in drafting, his responses to questions in press conferences and in townhall meetings, and comments made by his closest associates that have appeared in public media. I give less attention to prepared campaign speeches, presidential remarks to various groups, and formal addresses that Obama has given that have been drafted in whole or large part by others. As much as possible, I let Obama speak for himself.

NOTES

1. For contemporary reviews of personality theory, see Gregory J. Boyle, Gerald Matthews, and Donald H. Saklofske, eds., *The SAGE Handbook of Personality Theory and Assessment* (Los Angeles: Sage Publications, 2008); Albert Ellis, Mike Abrams, with Lidia Abrams, *Personality Theories: Critical Perspectives* (Los Angeles: Sage Publications, 2009); and Robert B. Ewan, *An Introduction to Theories of Personality*, 7th ed. (New York: Psychology Press, 2010).
2. Richard E. Neustadt, *Presidential Power* (New York: Free Press, 1991).
3. In a study of roll call votes in five major issue areas between 1953 and 1964, Aage R. Clausen discovered presidential influence in only one of them, international intervention. Aage R. Clausen, *How Congressmen Decide* (New York: St. Martin's Press, 1973). John W. Kingdon interviewed members of Congress and their staffs who reported relatively little presidential influence compared with the influence that they claimed fellow members and their own constituents exerted on them. Kingdon, *Agendas, Alternatives, and Public Policies* (Boston: Little, Brown, 1984). Similarly, presidential scholar George C. Edwards III's study of congressional roll calls on which presidents took positions concluded that presidents regarded as most skillful did not receive more support from members of Congress than those reputed to be less skillful. On the basis of his analysis, Edwards concludes that presidents tend to be influential at the margins, not on most votes of most legislators on most issues. Edwards, *At the Margins* (New Haven, Conn.: Yale University Press, 1989). Jon Bond and Richard Fleisher also found little systemic evidence to support the exercise of influence in Congress by the president. Bond and Fleisher, *The President in the Legislative Arena* (Chicago: University of Chicago Press, 1990).
4. See the references in note 1 for a discussion of these theories.
5. See, for example, John R. Alford, Carolyn L. Funk, and John R. Hibbing, "Are Political Orientations Genetically Transmitted?" *American Political Science Review*, 99 (2005): 153–67; and James H. Fowler, Laura A. Baker, and Christopher T. Dawes, "Genetic Variation in Political Participation," *American Political Science Review*, 102 (2008): 233–48.

6. James David Barber in his book on presidential character suggested that there was a preferential character type. He believed that people who were most active and gained the most satisfaction from their work make the best presidents. He referred to this type as Active-Positive.

Barber's belief was based on a normative view of the office that suggests being active contributes to the energy needed to do the job and being positive eases the inevitable interpersonal conflicts that result from competing perspectives, interests, policy goals, and ambitions of the president and those around him or her.

Most political scientists criticized this view. They regarded it as overly simplistic and judgmental. They pointed to great presidents, such as Lincoln and Theodore Roosevelt, who did not fit the model, and to less highly regarded presidents, such as Ford, Carter, and George H. W. Bush, who did. *The Presidential Character: Predicting Presidential Performance in the White House* (Englewood Cliffs, NJ: Prentice Hall, 1972), 11–14.

7. Barber, *The Presidential Character*, 5.

8. Stanley A. Renshon, *The Psychological Assessment of Presidential Candidates* (New York: Routledge, 1998), 184.

9. Ibid., 186–88.

10. Fred I. Greenstein, *The Presidential Difference* (New York: Free Press, 2000), 108–09, 188, 199–200.

11. Robert Barnes and Michael D. Shear, "McCain: Fundamentals of Economy are 'Strong' But 'Threatened,'" *Washington Post*, September 18, 2008, http://voices.washingtonpost.com/44/2008/09/15/mccain_fundamentals_of_economy.html.

12. Jonathan Alter, *The Promise* (New York: Simon & Schuster, 2010), 10–14.

13. According to David Axelrod, Obama's principal media adviser during the campaign, "We used the word 'erratic' a lot during that period. . . . Our feeling was that there was a herky-jerky nature to what was going on at the time and it played well against our solidarity." Quoted in Kathleen Hall Jamieson, ed. *Electing the President 2008: The Insiders' View* (Philadelphia: University of Pennsylvania Press, 2009), 75.

14. Renshon, *Psychological Assessment of Presidential Candidates*, 188–90.

15. Barack Obama, *The Audacity of Hope* (New York: Crown, 2006), 45.

16. Barber, *Presidential Character*, 10.

1

CHARACTER DEVELOPMENT

"I was trying to raise myself to be a black man in America and beyond the given of my appearance, no one around me seemed to know exactly what that meant."

—Obama, *Dreams from My Father*[*]

"I was different, after all, potentially suspect; I had no idea who my own self was."

—Obama, *Dreams from My Father*[*]

"I have brothers, sisters, nieces, nephews, uncles and cousins, of every race and every hue, scattered across three continents, and for as long as I live, I will never forget that in no other country on Earth is my story even possible."

—Obama, "A More Perfect Union"[*]

Barack Obama thinks of himself as an African American, the son of an African father and American mother. His duel ancestry has given him the credentials, experience, and desire to bridge the racial divide in ways that most Americans, black or white, can not. Because of his background,

---

[*]Barack Obama, *Dreams from My Father* (New York: Three Rivers Press, 1995), 76.

[*]Ibid., 82.

[*]Obama, "A More Perfect Union," March 18, 2008.

Obama believes that he can understand and empathize with the struggles, attitudes, and feelings of Americans of all races, which is the reason that he begins his campaign speeches with his life story:

> I am the son of a black man from Kenya and a white woman from Kansas. I was raised with the help of a white grandfather who survived a Depression to serve in Patton's Army during World War II and a white grandmother who worked on a bomber assembly line at Fort Leavenworth while he was overseas.
>
> I've gone to some of the best schools in America and lived in one of the world's poorest nations. I am married to a black American who carries within her the blood of slaves and slaveowners—an inheritance we pass on to our two precious daughters.
>
> I have brothers, sisters, nieces, nephews, uncles and cousins, of every race and every hue, scattered across three continents, and for as long as I live, I will never forget that in no other country on Earth is my story even possible.[1]

Obama has used his diverse background to introduce his uniqueness as a candidate, to demonstrate his capacity to understand and empathize with the problems people face, to praise America, and to justify his political goals.

Race and Roots

That Obama categorizes himself as African American is a consequence of his skin color, his mixed racial ancestry, and the belittling and discrimination he personally experienced growing up in a race-conscious America.[2] In *Dreams from My Father,* he writes about his first day at Punahou Academy in Hawaii after his return from Indonesia, when students mocked his name and his African ancestry. "A redheaded girl asked to touch my hair and seemed hurt when I refused. A ruddy-faced boy asked me if my father ate people."[3]

In *The Audacity of Hope* he wrote,

> I can recite the usual litany of petty slights that during my forty-five years have been directed my way: security guards tailing me as I shop in department stores, white couples who toss me their car keys as I stand outside a restaurant waiting for the valet, police cars pulling me over for no apparent reason. I know what it's like to have people tell me I can't do something because of my color, and I know the bitter swill of swallowed-black anger.[4]

The young Obama's conscious association with African Americans, beginning in his middle school years, reinforced his growing racial identity, his perceptions of discrimination, and his search for community—all of which contributed to his identity decisions.[5]

During this period of his life, Obama strove to be like other African Americans his age. He adopted what he perceived to be their mannerisms, their likes (sports, especially basketball) and dislikes (hitting the books hard). In later years he reflected on his experience in an article he wrote for his high school alumni magazine:

> As an African-American teenager in a school with few African-Americans, I probably questioned my identity a bit harder than most. As a kid from a broken home and family of relatively modest means, I nursed more resentment than my circumstances justified, and didn't always channel those resentments in particularly constructive ways.[6]

Young Barack with his mother, Ann Dunham Obama.

Added to this racial identity quest was the personal challenge of succeeding as an African American in a society dominated by whites. Obama
did not want his acceptance and achievements diminished by his maternal
ancestry. "I ceased to advertise my mother's race at the age of twelve or
thirteen, when I began to suspect that by doing so I was ingratiating myself
to whites. . . ."[7]

Embracing the African American experience, growing up, trying to figure out his identity, and subsequently writing of his struggle to do so,
Obama's coming of age is the story of an adolescent and young man, finding and accepting himself for who he was and what he overcame. He saw
his struggle as unique and surmounting the hurdles that threatened to
define and limit him as extraordinary and extemporary, so much so that he
wrote about them.

That Obama believed his life experience, his trials and tribulations, to be
so different and of such interest that they would engage the attention of
others is evidence of considerable grandiosity and self-conceit. Moreover,
in telling his story in *Dreams from My Father,* Obama embellishes his nar-
rative with such detail and conveys such strong emotions that some of the
real world subjects in the manuscript indicated to reporters that Obama's
description of personalities and events were exaggerated.[8] Subsequently, in
middle age, running for president, Obama seemed a little embarrassed by
the raw feelings he expressed and impetuous actions he described in the
book. He attributes the emotions he felt and the activities in which he
engaged in his teen years to being "an adolescent male with a lot of hor-
mones and an admittedly complicated upbringing."[9]

Obama evidences little anger in public life today.[10] In fact, he seems to
repress his emotions. He is amazingly self-disciplined and self-confident.
He needs to be in control, keeps his grandiosity, which he retains, under
wraps, and displays a cool rationality.

The Obama running for elected office seemed comfortable with himself
and his mixed racial heritage; he wore that heritage as a mantra, a badge of
social acceptance, much to the dismay of some older African American
leaders who have complained that he is not "black enough," and that he
somehow talks down to people of his own race.[11]

Obama is careful not to project himself as a typical African American
politician. In his own words, "I'm rooted in the African-American community, but not limited by it."[12] Throughout his career he has demonstrated
that he is not a traditional politician, that his diverse background enables
him to understand and appreciate the plight of a large cross-section of

Americans. His appeal has been to a new generation; he projects a new image, a person who has moved beyond race to resemble what America has become, a multiracial society in which racial and ethnic minorities can aspire to achieve the American Dream just like those in the white, Anglo majority. He has combined that appeal with a "can do" mentality.

Obama is both the model for the "can do" dream as well as the preacher who paved the way. During his 2008 presidential campaign, he is the messenger but also the person who personifies the message. To get to that point, however, he had to work to rid himself of resentment toward an absent and irresponsible father and perhaps also to a mother who pursued her own career goals doing research in Indonesia (to earn a Ph.D. in Anthropology) while her only son returned to Hawaii to live with his maternal grandparents.

His yearning to discover his roots was evident from the time Obama first realized he was different. He talks about his teen years and his experience of "the constant, crippling fear that I didn't belong somehow, that unless I dodged and hid and pretended to be something I wasn't, I would forever remain an outsider, with the rest of the world, black and white, always standing in judgment."[13]

Searching for roots to claim as his own was a necessary, arduous, and painful task for young Obama, heightened not only by his mixed racial ancestry and the absence of his African father but also by his mother's second marriage to a man from Indonesia and the five years Obama spent living in that country from the age of six to ten. His was a persistent search for identity, one in which he first tried to acknowledge and accept his blackness, then his African ancestry, subsequently his religious commitment and community, and finally his brand of Americanism.

Finding roots is an important part of self-understanding for most people. It helps define who we are and what we value and believe. For Obama, roots provided him with a sense of belonging, a heritage from which he could explain his thinking, reactions and emotions, and eventually, aspirations. In his own words, "I am a prisoner of my own biography: I can't help but view the American experience through the lens of a black man of mixed heritage. . . ."[14]

Roots also helped the young Obama ground himself in reality, aiding him in severing the fantasies he created as a child, his dreams about his father. Roots provided a foundation on which he could stand and appreciate how the culture and tradition of racial, ethnic, and religious groups contributed to the fabric of American society. These roots and that appreciation helped him to avoid the escapism in which his grandfather, father, and mother engaged and the loneliness that followed from it for each of them.[15] By realizing his ties to others, roots helped free him from his own loneliness and helped him to define and accept himself. It gave him an identity and community.

The desire for sturdy roots is one reason Michelle Obama and her family were so attractive to Barack. They were the stable, close-knit African American family he never had and, over time, had wanted so much. Her parents understood their heritage. They had their own family stories that traced their lineage back to slavery in America. They were part of the great migration of African Americans to the urban centers following World War II, a tight-knit family that provided for itself. Hard-working and responsible, Michelle's parents gave their children opportunities they never had. Both Michelle and her brother attended Princeton as undergraduates, and Michelle earned a law degree from Harvard.

In addition to providing brethren and tradition, a community of shared history, common values, a sense of belonging, roots also may have satisfied another personal need for Obama—the need to contain his own grandiosity by placing himself within a larger and less self-centered environment. Growing up in a household of three adults, with no appropriate male role model[16] and without a sibling for his first six years, Obama was likely indulged, probably not materially—the family was of modest means—but more likely emotionally. The attention lavished on him as a young child may have enlarged his perceptions of his own importance, evident in the publication of his early life story at the ripe old age of 33.

Throughout his writings and in his campaign speeches, Obama constantly reminds himself of his enlarged ego, his "relentless" ambition and his self-centeredness. That reminder, both in speeches and in print, has had political benefits as well. It has made him seem more conscious of his own ego, and as a consequence, more personable, with ambitions with which people could identify. To interviewer David Remnick of *The New Yorker,* Obama said, "I try to take to heart, and that is to make sure that, whatever it is that I do, that I'm not solely driven by what's inside of me, but also by what the country needs. . . ."[17]

Ambition and Politics

Obama is a very ambitious person, albeit one who has camouflaged that ambition with his rational discourse, cool temperament, and the social goals that he claims motivated or at least justified his political pursuits. He believes that his ambition ". . . was fueled by my father—by my knowledge of his achievements and failures, by my unspoken desire to somehow earn his love and by my resentments and anger toward him," although he credits his mother with providing him with the direction that he desired those ambitions to take. She saw the goodness of people, their humanity, what Obama sees, claims, and justifies for his political drives.[18]

Political ambition and the political channel through which he has sought to pursue it led to Obama's interest first in political philosophy and international relations in college and then to the real-world experience of community organizing. After he became aware of the difficulties of changing conditions from the ground up, he decided to go to law school to get the knowledge and credentials he would need to change them from the top down. Despite opportunities to practice with prominent Chicago firms, he chose to join a small civil rights law firm. He also began to make the connections to foster a political career. He saw power and position as critical to the achievement of his personal and social goals.

Throughout his life, Obama has been driven to set goals for himself and then achieve and exceed them. He was smart enough to get by in high school as he sorted out his identity and looked for a community. Once he put his mind to it, he excelled in college and later at Harvard Law School, the same university that his father attended as a graduate student. The young Obama successfully politicked to get elected president of the *Harvard Law Review* and used the status and the notoriety he received as the first African American to hold that position to get a book contract, an office for writing it, and later a teaching position at the University of Chicago Law School. At Harvard and Chicago, he also set about making the personal connections he would need to further his political career.

Obama creates and takes advantage of opportunities. Abandoned by his biological father before birth and sent back to Hawaii from Indonesia at the age of 10 to live with his white grandparents and attend a prestigious school, he has learned to be self-sufficient. Never content to rest on his laurels, he attributes his drive to ". . . either the absence or the presence of a father who ends up motivating you in some way."[19] Obama's philosophy has always been to strike while the iron is hot, but he has certainly contributed to its heating by carefully and relentlessly calculating his every political move.

There's a toughness about him, a steeliness, that is masked by his conciliatory attitude, easy manner, and polished style but also hardened by experience in Chicago politics. Push him to the brink, he fights back forcibly, a lesson that he attributes to his stepfather. In *Dreams from My Father,*

Obama tells the story of a fight he had with an older boy who threw a rock that hit him in the head. The next day his stepfather brought home two boxing gloves and taught the young Obama how to defend himself.[20] He remembered his stepfather's advice, "better to be strong," and has practiced it ever since.[21]

In situations in which his political ambitions have been directly challenged, as they were by former Illinois representative Alice Palmer, Rev. Jeremiah Wright, and indirectly by his pledge to accept government funds for the general election if his Republican opponent did the same, Obama responded forcefully and unequivocally. When Illinois state legislator Alice Palmer, whose seat he was seeking in 1996, asked him to step aside after she was defeated in the Democratic primary for Congress, he refused to do so and went so far as to challenge the signatures on her petition to get on the ballot, a challenge that was successful.

When the Rev. Jeremiah Wright defended what Obama described as incendiary remarks Wright made at a speech at the National Press Club, Obama repudiated the reverend and cut his ties with a man he considered a personal and family friend, a person who had presided over Obama's marriage, baptized him and his children, and with whom he had socialized on occasions.

As a candidate for the Democratic Party's presidential nomination, Obama indicated that he would accept federal funds for the general election if his Republican opponent did the same. Nonetheless, he opted out of this pledge when he realized that he would have a significant fund-raising advantage with private funding.

When it comes to his political ambitions, Obama lets little stand in the way of achieving his personal goals. Conciliation is replaced by determination, and if need be, confrontation. He is extremely competitive.

Adaptation and Approval

Obama is a master at understanding and assimilating into the environments in which he finds himself. His years of coping with his mixed racial identity in Hawaii, living as a small boy in a nonwestern country (Indonesia), and trying to discover himself at a private, elite high school and two distant and somewhat dissimilar college environments in Los Angeles (Occidental College) and New York City (Columbia University) created a need for adaptive skills that he mastered at a young age and has artfully used since then to further his professional career and his political ambitions.

Source: Reuters/Obama For America/Handout (United States) US Presidential Election Campaign 2008 (USA)

Obama with his grandparents in New York City during the time that he was an undergraduate student at Columbia University.

Put him into a distinctive culture and he adapts, using his cognitive, language, and social skills to blend in and move up. He enters new political environments by playing the role of apprentice, learning from those who have knowledge and power. He listens and learns. His initial impulse is to lay low and work hard. He pulls his weight, and eventually gains recognition for his attitude, intelligence, industry, and achievements. Over the years this behavioral pattern has produced mentors, colleagues, and others who sing his praises, testifying to his exceptional talent, skills, and resolve.

In the Illinois Senate, he worked closely with Emil Jones, the Democratic minority leader in 1997, the year Obama became a state senator; in the U.S. Senate, it was more of the same. He learned from Majority Leader Harry Reid, long-time senator and master of that institution's parliamentary rules, Harry Byrd, and Ted Kennedy. He crossed the aisle to sponsor bills with several Republicans. Similarly, as a candidate for office, he perfected his speaking style with help from experienced campaign operatives.[22] In each case, Obama shrewdly planned his behavior with his personal and political goals in mind. He left little to chance, and it paid off.

Once he understands how people interact within their environment, the strategies and tactics they use, the behavior that is appropriate, and traditions they observe, he joins the game, be it in the back rooms of

Chicago politics, poker with state legislative leaders—Obama learned golf to broaden his knowledge and contacts—or national electoral campaigns. He adapts easily and relatively quickly to new situations. This skill has enabled him to claim a broad understanding of and generate an appeal to a cross-section of Americans.

Being seen, heard, and categorized as a minority is inherently limiting politically in the United States, the reason Obama has moved beyond being associated with one particular group. He sees his roots as multiple and has used them to maximize his political appeal, be it in the mixed racial Hyde Park community, the state of Illinois, and—beginning in 2004 with his keynote address at the Democratic National Convention—the entire country. The success with which he has been able to become part of mainstream America has led some seasoned politicians to comment about his multiracial appeal. Sen. Joe Biden got it right but said it wrong, or at least politically inappropriately, at the beginning of the 2007–2008 nomination cycle when he described Obama as ". . . the first mainstream African-American who is articulate and bright and clean and a nice-looking guy."[23] Similarly, Senate majority leader Harry Reid referred to Obama as "light-skinned with no Negro dialect, unless he wanted to have one."[24] Obama himself admits, "I learned to slip back and forth between my black and white worlds, understanding that each possessed its own language and customs and structures of meaning, convinced that with a bit of translation on my part the two worlds would eventually cohere."[25]

One of Obama's most impressive skills is language: accent and cadence. Biographer David Remnick writes that Obama "was adept at pitching his cadences one way in black churches, another way at a P.T.A. meeting downstate, and yet another at a living-room gathering in [Chicago's] Hyde Park or the near North Side."[26]

Obama appears to get a high from politics, despite his disclaimers to the contrary.[27] He seems exhilarated by the crowds he draws, feels "cleansed" by his interaction with every day folks,[28] and glorifies in the virtue of his message.[29] He has described his presidency initially as "exhilarating."

He has been captured by the passion of his own message—unifying America, renewing its spirit, and providing greater and better opportunities to more people. He saw in his inauguration a powerful affirmation of the possibilities in America for everyone. He thinks of his triumphs in symbolic terms and sees great opportunities to improve conditions for everyone, particularly those who need it the most and have the least capacity to help themselves.

The danger for Obama is one to which he has succumbed—creating unrealistic expectations that cannot be easily met, a danger he noted in *The Audacity of Hope:*

> I am new enough on the national political scene that I serve as a blank screen on which people of vastly different political stripes project their own views. As such, I am bound to disappointment some, if not all, of them. Which perhaps indicates a second, more intimate theme to this book [*The Audacity of Hope*]—namely, how I or anybody in public office, can avoid the pitfalls of fame, the hunger to please, the fear of loss, and thereby retain that kernel of truth, that singular voice within each of us that reminds us of our deepest commitments.[30]

Despite these cautions, of which he reminds himself with some regularity, particularly on the campaign trail,[31] he continued to pursue his political ambitions in a carefully calculated, almost compulsive manner, and preach an uplifting, open-ended message of transformational politics and policy.[32] That message and the optimism associated with it has created difficulties for his presidency.

Obama needs to be recognized. He wants to make a difference. Politics provides a salve for his ego, a direction for his restlessness, a channel through which he can achieve desirable social goals. He admits getting caught up in it, spending 12 to 16 hours a day, with little or no break, on his campaign for the Democratic nomination for U.S. Senate from Illinois, then as Democratic candidate for president, and later as president. It is unclear whether he finds that effort pleasurable or necessary or both.

He writes in the third person in *The Audacity of Hope* that politicians often lose their bearings in their quest for elective office, adversely affecting their own "health, relationship, mental balance, and dignity," leaving his reader to guess the extent to which he has fallen victim to this particular social illness.[33] He admitted at least indirectly to his unusually high level of ambition that fueled his subsequent behavior when he noted to interviewer Jon Meacham, "You could argue that if you're too well adjusted, you don't end up running for president."[34] On ABC News in 2007 he said, "If you don't have enough self-awareness to see the element of megalomania involved in thinking you should be President, then you probably shouldn't be President. There's a slight madness to thinking you should be the leader of the free world."[35]

His loss in the 2000 Democratic primary to Rep. Bobby Rush pained him deeply. In *The Audacity of Hope,* he wrote, "I still burn . . . with the thought of my one loss in politics."[36] Despite the loss, however, he continued, even accelerated his quest for higher and higher elective office, launching his campaign for the U.S. Senate two years later. After being in the Senate for only two years, he began preparations for a presidential run, taking on Democratic frontrunner Hillary Rodham Clinton without the large war chest, endorsements, and political machinery that she had. In the words of Illinois state senator Donne Trotter, "You would look at him and say, 'Oh, he's pretty relaxed kind of guy. You know, he's easy to get along with.' But if you take a hard look at him, you'll see that there's an intensity in his eyes. He doesn't like to lose."[37]

Ego Checks and Guilt

Obama realizes his extraordinary ambition. He regularly cautions himself in public, particularly when running for office, ostensibly to prevent his own and public expectations surrounding him from getting out of hand. Such warnings, whether written or expressed, are also good politics. They have enabled him to seem more publicly motivated and less personally ambitious than most stereotypical politicians. They have also allowed him to project a more pristine image.

In a 2004 interview with *Chicago Sun Times* religious correspondent, Cathleen Falsani, he said,

> There's a vanity aspect to politics, and then there's a substantive part of politics. . . . I think it's easy to get swept up in the vanity side of it, the desire to be liked and recognized and important. It's important to me throughout the day to measure and to take stock and to say, now, am I doing this business because I think it's advantageous to me politically, or because I think it's the right thing to do? Am I doing this to get my name in the papers, or am I doing this because it's necessary to accomplish my motives?[38]

In much the same vein, he wrote in *The Audacity of Hope,*

> I may tell myself that in some larger sense I am in politics for Malia and Sasha [his daughters], that the work I do will make the world a better place for them. But such rationalizations seem feeble and painfully

abstract when I'm missing one of the girls' school's potluck dinners because of a vote, or calling Michelle to tell her that session's been extended and we need to postpone our vacation.[39]

Away from home for extended periods while campaigning for public office and then serving in those offices, Obama has indicated that he feels particularly guilty about the sacrifices his family has made to further his political career. In his books and speeches, he recalls again and again how his wife and family bring him back to reality. Obviously, he feels guilty about pursuing his ambitions at their expense, particularly in the light of his perception that his parents pursued theirs at his expense. "I determined that my father's irresponsibility toward his children, my stepfather's remoteness, and my grandfather's failures would all become object lessons for me, and that my own children would have a father they could count on."[40] After claiming that his marriage was successful and his family provided for, he then added, "And yet, of all the areas of my life, it is in my capacities as a husband and father that I entertain the most doubt."[41]

In addition to reiterating his own anxieties, Obama included a description of his wife's unhappiness in *The Audacity of Hope*:

Source: © Jason Reed/Reuters/Corbis

President Obama, his wife, and daughters at the Easter Egg Roll at the White House.

". . . we had little time for conversation, much less romance. When I launched my ill-fated congressional run, Michelle put up no pretense of being happy with the decision . . ." Obama painfully recounted her criticism: "You only think of yourself," she would tell me, adding, "I never thought I would have to raise a family alone."[42]

Rather than defending himself, he acknowledges Michelle's criticism and compensates for her sacrifices by lavishing praise on her heroics and putting her on a pedestal.[43] In the same vein, he wrote about his eldest child, ". . . it gives me small comfort to think that my eight-year-old daughter loves me enough to overlook my shortcomings."[44] Living in the White House with his family and mother-in-law has minimized the guilt he felt about pursuing his ambitions at his family's expense. He usually has breakfast and dinner with them when he is at the White House and has taken the family on several trips abroad.

In sum, in his writings and campaign speeches, Obama recognizes his own ambition and the sacrifices that others have made on his behalf, his mother and grandparents and his wife and children. He cautions himself not to let the personal dimensions of his quest for position, power, and notoriety get out of hand. He sees himself and his family as the most effective constraints on his own self-interested behaviors. Yet he continues to believe his political pursuits are justified because they serve larger social goals, particularly helping those who have not had the opportunities he had to achieve their dreams and aspirations.

Summary

Obama struggled with his biracial heritage; an absent father and, for a time, absent mother; a transient upbringing; and all the emotions these conditions generated in his teenage and early adult years. He overcame these self-perceived deficiencies by compensating for what he had missed by immersing himself in a variety of experiences in the African American community. At the same time, he realized the limitations of these experiences by reaching beyond them with more education, professional training, and political contacts.

Today, Obama looks at his roots as a foundation on which to build. He sees his diversity as a strength to be touted, a uniqueness that distinguishes him from other politicians, one that enables him to understand and appreciate the needs and aspirations of a broad cross-section of Americans.

Critical to his political success has been his adaptive skills. He is a learner, a listener, and a conciliator. His ability to adjust to new environments has contributed to his self-confidence; his ease in confronting new positions and situations; and his steadiness, temperament, and relaxed style. That ability has also fostered the challenges on which Obama desires to focus his relentless energy and satisfy his grandiose political goals.

He leaves little to chance. He calculates, using his considerable intelligence to figure out complex policy problems and political issues. He works hard, driven by personal ambition, a need to succeed and excel. These attributes have enabled him to move up the achievement ladder quickly. His is a political success story that he sees in instrumental and social terms as steps on America's long road toward equality. He believes his story exemplifies and exceptionalizes the American experience. That perspective, along with bumps in the road and the realities of everyday life, helps Obama keep himself in check.

NOTES

1. Barack Obama, "A More Perfect Union," March 18, 2008.
2. Barack Obama, *Dreams from My Father* (New York: Three Rivers Press, 1995), 60, 80. During his 2008 presidential campaign, Obama frequently referred to his mixed racial heritage, a fact obviously intended to enhance his acceptability among white voters. Growing up, however, he sought roots and community, both of which the African American tradition in the United States provided. Obama's association with African Americans during his teenage and early adult years reinforced his identity as an African American, which is how he thinks of himself today.
3. Ibid., 60.
4. Barack Obama, *The Audacity of Hope* (New York: Crown, 2006), 233.
5. Obama, *Dreams*, 72–129.
6. David Remnick, *The Bridge* (New York: Knopf, 2010), 92.
7. Obama, *Dreams*, xv.
8. Kirstein Scharnberg and Kim Barker, "The Not-So-Simple Story of Barack Obama's Youth," *Chicago Tribune,* March 25, 2007, www.chicagotribune.com/news/politics/obama/chi-070325obama-youth-story-archive,0.
9. Larissa MacFarquhar, "The Conciliator," *New Yorker,* May 7, 2007, 50. www.newyorker.com/reporting/2007/05/07/070507fa_fact_macfarquhar.

10. Both he and his wife acknowledge the catharsis he felt in writing *Dreams from My Father*. It drained his emotion and kept him on the even keel he has demonstrated since the book was completed.

11. In the words of Jesse Jackson's ill-fated comment on *Fox & Friends,* a Sunday morning news show on the Fox News, "Barack, he's talking down to black people. I want to cut his nuts off." Matea Gold, "Jackson Apologizes for Crude Remark about Obama," *Los Angeles Times,* July 10, 2008, www.chicagotribune .com/news/politics/obama/chi-070325obama-youth-story-archive,0.

12. Remnick, *The Bridge,* 382.

13. Obama, *Dreams,* 111.

14. Obama, *Audacity,* 10.

     Interestingly, Obama explains his empathy with Israel in terms of the importance of roots. ". . . the idea of Israel and the reality of Israel is one that I find important to me personally. Because it speaks to my history of being unrooted, it speaks to the African American story of Exodus, it describes the history of overpowering great odds and a courage and commitment to carving out a democracy and prosperity in the midst of hardscrabble land." Jeffrey Goldberg, "Obama on Zionism and Hamas," *TheAtlantic.com,* May 12, 2008, http:// www.chicagotribune.com/news/politics/obama/chi-070325obama-youth-story-archive,0. Obama sees the existence of the state of Israel as a rebirth, much like the struggles of colonial Africa.

15. Barack Obama, *Dreams,* 16, 17, 21, 50–51, 439.

16. In *The Audacity of Hope* he wrote,

    There were men in my life—a stepfather with whom we lived for four years, and my grandfather, who along with my grandmother helped raise me the rest of the time—and both were good men who treated me with affection. But my relationships with them were necessarily partial and incomplete. In the case of my stepfather, this was a result of limited duration and his natural reserve. And as close as I was to my grandfather, he was both too old and too troubled to provide me with much direction. Obama, *Audacity,* 346.

17. David Remnick, "Testing the Waters," *New Yorker,* November 6 2006, www .newyorker.com/archive/2006/10/30on_onlineonly04?currentPage=3.

18. Obama, *Audacity,* 205–06.

19. Jon Meacham, "Transcript of Obama Interview," *Newsweek,* September 1, 2008, 32.

20. Obama, *Dreams,* 35–36.

21. Ibid., 41.

22. Biographer David Remnick writes, "After countless speeches, cocktail parties, panel discussions, fund-raising dinners, business lunches, and state fairs, after speaking in the pulpits of black churches in Chicago and in V.F.W. halls downstate, he had become a better orator, a smoother campaigner, a more

disciplined fundraiser. Obama was beginning to develop his signature appeal, the use of details of his own life as a reflection of a kind of multicultural ideal, a conceit both sentimental and effective." Remnick, *The Bridge,* 360.

23. Xuan Thai and Ted Barrett, "Biden's Description of Obama Draws Scrutiny," CNN News, February 9, 2007, www.cnn.com/2007/,POLITICS/01/31/biden .obama.

24. John Heilemann and Mark Halperin, *Game Change* (HarperCollins, 2010), 36.

25. Remnick, *The Bridge,* 240. When Obama recorded the audio for his book, *Dreams from My Father,* he adopted the accents of his characters as he reads his story.

26. Remnick, *The Bridge,* 361.

27. ". . . the older I get, the less important feeding my vanity becomes. I've discovered that I don't get a lot of satisfaction from being the center of attention, but I do get a lot of satisfaction about getting work done." Jann S. Wenner, "A Conversation with Barack Obama," *Rolling Stone,* July 10, 2008, www.jannswenner .com/Archives/Barack_Obama.aspx.

28. Remnick, *The Bridge,* 102.

29. Ibid., 8–9.

30. Obama, *Audacity,* 11.

31. Obama, *Audacity,* 105.

32. Ryan Lizza describes Obama's nonstop quest for public office in an article in the *New Yorker* in 2008. In that article, Lizza reports that Obama was planning his political career from the time he returned to Chicago in the early 1990s. "Obama was writing '*Dreams*' at the moment that he was preparing for a life in politics, and he launched his book and his first political campaign simultaneously, in the summer of 1995, when he saw his first chance of winning." Lizza, "Making It," *New Yorker,* July 21, 2008, 53. www.newyorker.com/reporting/ 2008/07/21/080721fa_fact_lizza.

Lizza details in his article the steps Obama took and the acquaintances he made to further his political ambitions.

33. Obama, *Audacity,* 105.

34. Meacham, "Obama Interview, 32."

35. ABC World News, November 1, 2007.

36. Obama, *Audacity,* 105.

37. Margaret Warner, "PBS Interviews with Obama's Campaign Aides," *Public Broadcasting System News Hour,* September 23, 2008.

38. Cathleen Falsani, "Obama Interview," *Chicago Sun Times* March 27, 2004, http://blog.beliefnet.com/stevenwaldman/2008/11/obamas-interview-with-cathleen.html.

39. Obama, *Audacity,* 348.

40. Ibid., 346.

41. Ibid.

42. Ibid., 340.
43. "She is smart, funny, and thoroughly charming. She is also very beautiful, although not in a way that men find intimidating or women find off-putting; it is the lived-in beauty of the mother and busy professional rather than the touched-up image we see on the cover of the glossy magazines." Ibid., 327. Michelle is the first to be lauded in most of his speeches and in the acknowledgments of his book, *The Audacity of Hope:* "With each passing day, I understand more fully just how lucky I am to have Michelle in my life, and can only hope that my boundless love for her offers some consolation for my constant preoccupations." Obama, *Audacity,* 363.
44. Obama, *Audacity,* 351.

2

BASIC BELIEFS

". . . we perfect our union by understanding that we may have different stories, but we hold common hopes; that we may not look the same and we may not have come from the same place, but we all want to move in the same direction—towards a better future for our children and grandchildren."

—Obama, "Speech on Racial Relations"[*]

". . . what I have come to understand is that regardless of your faith—and America is a country of Muslims, Jews, Christians, and non-believers—regardless of your faith, people have certain common hopes and common dreams."

—"President Obama's, Interview with Hisham Melham"[*]

"I think that more than anything is going to improve race relations, a sense of common progress, where everybody feels like they have a chance at the American Dream."

—Obama in Peter Nicolas, Christi Parsons, and John McCormick, "Text of Obama's First Newspaper Interview as President-Elect"[*]

---

[*]Barack Obama, "A More Perfect Union," March 18, 2008, blogs.wsj.com/washwire/2008/03/18/text-of-obamas-speech-a-more-perfect-union.

[*]"President Obama's Interview with Hisham Melham," January 26, 2009, www.america.gov/st/textrans-english/2009/January/20090127161320xjsnommis0.705578.html.

[*]Obama in Peter Nicolas, Christi Parsons, and John McCormick, "Text of Obama's First Newspaper Interview as President-Elect," *Los Angeles Times*, December 10, 2008, latimesblogs.latimes.com/washington/2008/12/obama-transcrip.html.

Obama's beliefs are a product of his identity quest. In his search for roots, he encountered diverse cultures, races, and ethnicities. He interacted with many of them, found roots in some of them, but came to the conclusion that in only one them, the United States of America, did he feel at home and believe that he could achieve his personal and social goals.

Obama's success as lawyer, educator, and elected official enhanced his appreciation for the American constitutional system and the protections it has provided for its citizens, especially those citizens who need it most: minorities; for the free enterprise, capitalistic system and the rewards it has provided for individual initiative, ingenuity, and effort; and the democratic political system, its representative character, and most important, its equalitarian values.

Obama is an equal-opportunity advocate. That advocacy initially prompted him to work directly with African Americans caught at the bottom of the socioeconomic ladder, using his education and personal skills to improve their plight first as a community organizer, then a civil rights attorney, state and national legislator, and finally as president.

Commonality as a Value

Obama's transient childhood combined with the absence of one or both parents for extended periods contributed to the importance he places on family, community, and country. He sees communal values as the glue that holds society together.[1] But he also sees the tensions that are created between the individual and the group and among groups.

> In every society (and in every individual), these twin strands—the individualist and the communal are in tension, and it has been one of the blessings of America that the circumstances of our nation's birth allowed us to negotiate these tensions better than most.[2]

America's big and sturdy tent is Obama's answer to the individual-community divide, a divide he encountered in his personal struggle to make sense of who he was, where he fit, what he believed, and how he could act on those beliefs.

Obama's social philosophy stems from his benevolent view of the American experience, an experience in which common values have woven a diverse population into a viable democracy, one that offers the promise of freedom and opportunity to all. This philosophy contributes to

Obama's penchant to be a conciliator and seek compromise, his constant search for common ground, and his campaign and governing message that Americans have more in common than the issues and ideologies that divide them.

His campaign oratory was optimistic. In 2008, he maintained a can-do attitude. In addition to being good politics when the public mood is sour, that attitude reflects his own success in furthering his professional and political career goals. As noted in Chapter 1, Obama sees himself as living testament to the reality and applicability of the American Dream, to the opportunity it offers others, and the obligations it demands of him as an advocate and role model to improve the plight of others.

He believes individual efforts on a national scale can cumulatively achieve a social transformation and quotes Ronald Reagan to that effect, ". . . we can shape our individual and collective destinies, so long as we rediscover the traditional values of hard work, patriotism, personal responsibility, optimism, and faith."[3] In his Inaugural address, Obama said,

> Our challenges may be new. The instruments with which we meet them may be new. But those values upon which our success depends—honesty and hard work, courage and fair play, tolerance and curiosity, loyalty and patriotism—these things are old. These things are true. They have been the quiet force of progress throughout our history.[4]

Obama repeats his common values, common interests, common ground litany again and again, at home and abroad. In his keynote address at the 2004 Democratic convention, he stated,

> . . . Alongside our famous individualism, there's another ingredient in the American saga, a belief that we are all connected as one people. . . . It is that fundamental belief—I am my brother's keeper, I am my sister's keeper—that makes this country work. It's what allows us to pursue our individual dreams, yet still come together as a single American family: "*E pluribus unum*"; out of many, one. . . . There's not a liberal America and a conservative America; there's the United States of America. There's not a black America and a white America and a Latino America and an Asian America; there's the United States of America. The pundits like to slice our country into red states and blue states. . . . But I've got news for them, too: We worship an awesome God in the blue states, and we don't

like federal agents poking around our libraries in the red states. We coach
Little League in the blue states, and yes, we've got some gay friends in the
red states.[5]

This "come together–stay together" refrain is found in most of Obama's
major campaign speeches, presidential addresses, and remarks intended
for international audiences.

> . . . we perfect our union by understanding that we may have different
> stories, but we hold common hopes; that we may not look the same and we
> may not have come from the same place, but we all want to move in the
> same direction—towards a better future for our children and grandchildren.[6]

> Our challenges may be new. The instruments with which we meet
> them may be new. But those values upon which our success depends—
> honesty and hard work, courage and fair play, tolerance and curiosity,
> loyalty and patriotism—these things are old . . . they have been the quiet
> force of progress throughout our history.[7]

> And the strongest democracies flourish from frequent and lively
> debate, but they endure when people of every background and belief find
> a way to set aside smaller differences in service of a greater purpose.[8]

> . . . when we open our hearts and our minds to those who may not
> think like we do or believe what we do—that's when we discover at least
> the possibility of common ground.[9]

> I've come here to Cairo to seek a new beginning between the United
> States and Muslims around the world, one based on mutual interest and
> mutual respect, and one based upon the truth that America and Islam are
> not exclusive and need not be in competition. Instead, they overlap, and
> share common principles—principles of justice and progress, tolerance
> and the dignity of human beings. . . . There must be a sustained effort to
> listen to each other; to learn from each other; to respect one another; and
> to seek common ground.[10]

Obama's optimism had a contagious quality to it during his 2008 presidential campaign, but in the light of the dire economic conditions that preceded his presidency and continued during his first and second years, that
optimism sounded out of place. The public remained dissatisfied, continued to believe the country was moving in the wrong direction, and lost confidence in Obama's ability to change it as indicated in the results of the
2010 midterm elections.[11]

Church and Community

Obama sees value in organized religion. It helps connect people to one another by establishing, maintaining, and extending the beliefs and practices that underlie most major religious faiths, beliefs and practices that Obama thinks are important because of their communal value. On a practical level, Obama, the community organizer, found the black churches to be the most valuable and dependable self-help groups on which he could depend. He also has noted on more than one occasion that churches were instrumental in providing the leadership and organizational capacity of the civil rights movement.[12]

It was not only the organizational support he saw as critical. It was the church's ability "to give people courage against great odds,"[13] hope that is so vitally a part of Obama's life experience and political message. Joining Trinity United Church of Christ in Chicago gave shape to his views on religion. It also was good politics for an aspiring politician who needed to firm up his African American base with personal contacts he could expand at this large and popular black congregation.[14]

From Obama's perspective, religion provides meaning in life and guidelines by which to live; it provides support that enables people to overcome personal tragedy. Obama sees spiritual faith as uplifting, "something that will relieve a chronic loneliness, . . . the assurance that somebody out there cares about them."[15]

The need for and desirability of this assurance lies behind Obama's much quoted, off-the-record comment during his 2008 presidential campaign about the bitterness felt by small–town, working-class voters who became frustrated with their economic plight:

> You go into some of these small towns in Pennsylvania, and like a lot of small towns in the Midwest, the jobs have been gone now for 25 years and nothing's replaced them. . . . . And it's not surprising then they get bitter, they cling to guns or religion or antipathy to people who aren't like them or anti-immigrant sentiment or anti-trade sentiment as a way to explain their frustrations.[16]

Although Obama thinks of himself as a person of faith, he writes that ". . . faith doesn't mean that you don't have doubts, or that you relinquish your hold on this world."[17] For him, the merits of religious beliefs lay less in the literal words of the Bible and more in the moral teachings it provides. "I think that religion at its best comes with a big dose of doubt. I'm suspicious of too much certainty in the pursuit of understanding just because I think people are limited in their understanding."[18]

Obama lauds Christ as a great teacher.

> Jesus is an historical figure for me, and he's also a bridge between God and man, in the Christian faith, and one that I think is powerful precisely because he serves as that means of reaching something higher.[19]

He attributes his own humanitarian beliefs to his mother, whom he describes as spiritual but not a churchgoer. "[H]er view always was that underlying these [the world's] religions, were a common set of beliefs about how you treat other people and how you aspire to act, not just for yourself but also for the greater good."[20] In *The Audacity of Hope*, he wrote, "There are certain things that I am absolutely sure about—the Golden rule, the need to battle cruelty in all its forms, the value of love and charity, humility and grace."[21]

Thus for Obama, religion provides community, tradition, and moral teachings. It also helps people to find meaning and contentment in their lives; it can help them overcome hardship; it extends their here and now. These values, which Obama claims that people derive from their religious traditions and beliefs, are reasons he expanded George W. Bush's faith-based initiative in the White House and why he does not support an absolute, high wall of separation between church and state. "Not every mention of God in public is a breach in the wall of separation; as the Supreme Court has properly recognized, context matters."[22]

> I know that as president, I want to celebrate the richness and diversity of our faith experience in this country. I think it is important for us to encourage churches and congregations all across the country to involve themselves in rebuilding communities.[23]

Obama's support for the right of a Muslim community to build a mosque and cultural center in New York City near the site of the terrorist attacks of 2001 is consistent with this belief in the communal value of organized religion. Obama, the constitutional scholar and law school professor, however, is more sensitive to the potential conflict between religious freedom and government activity.

> I am a big believer in the separation of church and state. I am a big believer in our constitutional structure. . . . I am a great admirer of our

founding charter, and its resolve to prevent theocracies from forming, and its resolve to prevent disruptive strains of fundamentalism from taking root in this country.[24]

"I'm very suspicious of religious certainty expressing itself in politics."[25] Similarly, he is critical of religious zealots who would impose their faith on others.[26] In a June 2007 address to a church convention, Obama said,

> Somehow, somewhere along the way, faith stopped being used to bring us together and started being used to drive us apart. It got hijacked. Part of it's because of the so-called leaders of the Christian Right, who've been all too eager to exploit what divides us.[27]
>
> I think there is an enormous danger on the part of public figures to rationalize or justify their actions by claiming God's mandate. I don't think it's healthy for public figures to wear religion on their sleeve as a means to insulate themselves from criticism, or dialogue with people who disagree with them.[28]

Obama was particularly angry with Alan Keyes, his Republican opponent in his 2006 Illinois Senate race, for presenting his views as God's truth, "with the certainty and fluency of an Old Testament prophet."[29] Recalling his difficulty of responding to Keyes' biblical arguments and to his allegations that Obama was not living a true Christian life, Obama notes that he frequently became "tongue-tied, irritable, and uncharacteristically tense" during his three debates with Keyes and even recalls one incident in which ". . . I poked him in the chest while making a point, a bit of alpha-male behavior that I hadn't engaged in since high school."[30]

Keyes may have reminded him of his father, also an assertive, strong-willed man who brooked no dissent. Throughout his adult life, Obama would rail against rash judgments, nondeliberative decision making, emotional responses, and instinctive reactions. As a law school professor, he would also challenge his students to understand the assumptions and perspectives that underlay their beliefs and the arguments that supported them.[31]

Obama's liberal voting record as a U.S. senator from Illinois and his support of expanded health care as president reflect his orientation to help the needy and his belief that government has an obligation to do so. If government does not create more equal opportunities, then who will?

Government and Society

"What are the core values that we, as Americans hold in common?" Obama asks in *The Audacity of Hope*.[32] He answers his own question by quoting Thomas Jefferson's words from the Declaration of Independence: "We hold these truths to be self-evident, that all men are created equal, that they are endowed by their Creator with certain unalienable Rights, that among these are Life, Liberty and the pursuit of Happiness."[33] These words, according to Obama, immortalize the American belief in individual freedom, the right to pursue one's own interests, a belief that he obviously shares with the caveat that he sees "self-interest . . . [as] linked to the interests of others."[34]

Obama places human rights and democracy high on his list of fundamental values. However, aware of the experience of the Bush administration that tried unsuccessfully to impose these values on Iraq after U.S. military action in 2003, he added, "I think it's a mistake for us to somehow suggest that we're not going to deal with countries around the world in the absence of their meeting all our criteria for democracy,"[35] a refrain that Secretary of State Hillary Rodham Clinton repeated in her first visit to China in 2009.

Constitutionalism and the Rule of Law

The tension between individual pursuits, group and community interests, and the society as a whole is moderated by law, enacted by elected representatives, implemented by appointed government officials and civil servants, and adjudicated by the courts. Obama views the rule of law as a fundamental, underlying tenet of American democracy. Law works to prevent tension between people and groups from getting out of hand. Government arbitrates differences. It does so on the basis of plurality rule, a fundamental principle of democracy, but one also predicated on the equality of all adult citizens. The Constitution secures the rights of all, including those in the minority. Its framework divides powers to make it more difficult for one group, majority or minority, to control authoritative decision making and, with that control, gain all the public policy outcomes they desire.

Obama the constitutional lawyer lauds that system even though he admits to its failure over the years to protect and promote the rights and interests of some groups: African Americans, women, Native Americans, Hispanics, and homosexuals. Nonetheless, he praises the Constitution as a framework by which individuals and groups within society can debate and resolve their differences; ". . . our democracy [is] not . . . a house to be built, but . . . a conversation to be had."[36]

Obama at Harvard Law School.

The Politics of Consensus

Consensus is the end game for Obama, not winning the debate or achieving a particular policy outcome. Reasoning together and arriving at a collective judgment is valuable because it bonds participants in a deliberative process, one that builds support for the policy because of the collective manner in which the decision is reached.

The public debate is continuous and the judgments and the resulting public policy must be adjusted as new information becomes available, new conditions emerge, and new beliefs begin to gain credibility among those who wish to convert them into practice. The disappointment, particularly for minorities, is that their inequities have persisted over a long period of time.

During the 2008 presidential campaign, racial inequalities were brought into the campaign when Rev. Jeremiah Wright's incendiary sermons in which he chastised America for its history of racism became public. After clips of the sermons found their way to the Internet, Obama first tried to distance himself from his minister's remarks and finally felt compelled to give a speech on race, the first and only one in his presidential campaign. Obama acknowledged the emotions and prejudice on both sides, suggesting that the true culprit of black anger and white resentment was economic policies that favored the few over the many: "a corporate culture rife with inside dealing, questionable accounting practices, and short-term greed; a Washington dominated by lobbyists and special interests."[37] He repeated this populist theme throughout the 2007–2008 campaign and during

his presidency to pinpoint responsibility as well as unify his diverse Democratic base.

Building and maintaining consensus through dialogue and diplomacy
also shape Obama's orientation toward the conduct of U.S. foreign policy.
"We should always strive to create coalitions—not coalitions that are
based on us twisting arms, withholding goodies, ignoring legitimate concerns of other countries, but coalitions that are based on a set of mutual
self-interests."[38] However, Obama has shown that he is not averse to committing forces as he has done in Afghanistan when persuasion alone
proves to be insufficient to achieve a critical national security goal.

Role of Government

Obama is a democratic leader and a capitalist. He believes that the political
and economic systems can and should reinforce each other. In his address to
a joint session of Congress during his first year in office, the president said,

> . . . our predecessors understood that government could not, and should
> not, solve every problem. They understood that there are instances when
> the gains in security from government action are not worth the added
> constraints on our freedom. But they also understood that the danger of
> too much government is matched by the perils of too little; that without
> the leavening hand of wise policy, markets can crash, monopolies can
> stifle competition, the vulnerable can be exploited.[39]

Obama sees a limited role for government, although this role is considerably more extensive than that of his contemporary Republican predecessors. He is fond of quoting Lincoln's dictum, "that we will do collectively,
through our government, only those things that we cannot do as well or at
all individually and privately."[40] However, Obama does not believe, as Reagan did, that government is the problem rather than the solution. On the
contrary, Obama sees government as a positive force in promoting greater
economic and social opportunities, especially for those at the lower end of
the socio-economic scale.

In defending his economic stimulus and reinvestment plan, Obama
said in an address to Congress:

> History reminds us that at every moment of economic upheaval and
> transformation, this nation has responded with bold action and big
> ideas. In the midst of civil war, we laid railroad tracks from one coast to
> another that spurred commerce and industry. From the turmoil of the

Industrial Revolution came a system of public high school that prepared our citizens for a new age. In the wake of war and depression the GI Bill sent a generation to college and created the largest middle-class in history, an American on the moon, and an explosion of technology that still shapes our world.

In each case, government didn't supplant private enterprise; it catalyzed private enterprise. It created conditions for thousands of entrepreneurs and new businesses to adapt and to thrive.[41]

In addition to being a catalyst for change, Obama also believes it is the responsibility of government to prevent economic, environmental, and social abuses from getting out of hand.[42] Like Democrats Roosevelt, Truman, and Johnson, Obama supports government regulation of an economy based on self-interested, profit-seeking behavior and a society in which income inequality has resulted in economic class distinctions.

Obama believes government must protect life's basic needs of food, shelter, and health care,[43] as well as prevent discriminatory actions that disadvantage the disadvantaged, , whether these actions be unequal pay for women; unequal rights for same-sex partners; or unequal treatment based on race, ethnicity, or religious affiliation. Obama's beliefs reflect his mother's humanism as well as his personal experience.

Speaking in Iowa in 2006, Obama said,

> You know, nobody here expects government to solve all our problems for us . . . but what we do expect is that government can help. That government can make a difference in all our lives and that is essentially the battle that we are going to be fighting in this election . . . a battle about what America is going to be.[44]

Obama supports using government to help reduce the inequality gap in income and opportunity through progressive taxes, tax credits, and direct benefits—food stamps, unemployment insurance, Medicaid, Medicare, Social Security, veterans' payments, and legislation to make health care insurance accessible to all Americans. His critics see government's redistribution of economic wealth as socialism; Obama sees it as fair play, as an important foundational component of the American Dream.

Obama articulated this role for government in his acceptance speech at the 2008 Democratic National Convention:

> Ours—ours is a promise that says government cannot solve all our problems, but what it should do is that which we cannot do for ourselves:

protect us from harm and provide every child a decent education; keep our water clean and our toys safe; invest in new schools, and new roads, and science, and technology.

Our government should work for us, not against us. It should help us, not hurt us. It should ensure opportunity not just for those with the most money and influence, but for every American who's willing to work.[45]

Finally, Obama believes government must act in times of crisis, a belief to which most of his predecessors have also subscribed. From his perspective, government was the only force capable of ". . . jolt[ing] the economy back to life,"[46] preventing even greater job losses, and rejuvenating the credit markets. When the 2010 oil spill in the Gulf of Mexico continued for more than a month, he said,

> I ultimately take responsibility for solving this crisis. I'm the President and the buck stops with me. So I give the people of this community and the entire Gulf my word that we're going to hold ourselves accountable to do whatever it takes for as long as it takes to stop this catastrophe, to defend our natural resources, to repair the damage, and to keep this region on its feet. Justice will be done for those whose lives have been upended by this disaster, for the families of those whose lives have been lost—that is a solemn pledge that I am making.[47]

During times of crisis, in the aftermath of the terrorist attacks of September 11, 2001, or the economic meltdown of 2008–2009, Congress generally supports presidential initiatives in which government plays a major role. It did for George W. Bush and has for Obama.

Role of the President
Obama sees his principal policy-making role as president as providing vision, not getting caught up in day-to-day politics.

> . . . one thing I'm pretty clear about is that as president, I've got to be looking out at the horizon. I can't be looking at today's headlines, because if I do, then I'm probably not going to make decisions based on what's best for the country. I'm going to be spending a lot of time worrying about day-to-day politics, and that's something I've been trying to block out.[48]

Coinciding with this view is a historical perspective that both justifies his change-oriented mantra as well as provides the excuse for not achieving it.

> Look, I think that there are certain moments in history where big change is possible . . . I think it's very hard to . . . for any single individual or politician to unleash historical momentum on its own. But I think when that historical wave is there, I think you can help guide it.[49]

During his 2008 campaign, Obama's focus on goals, not policy specifics, led to accusations that he was more poetry than substance, a charge he denied by pointing to his website, on which his proposals were discussed with greater specificity. He also demonstrated his detailed knowledge of policy issues during the presidential debates and as president privately during meetings with his advisers and publicly during press conferences, town meetings, and those teachable moments in which he assumed the role of educator in chief.

Obama working as a community organizer in Chicago.

Source: © Marc PoKempner. Originally published in *The New Yorker.*

Progressive Pragmatism

Obama is a pragmatist and a common-sense decision maker. He keeps his eye on the doable, not necessarily the optimal. Pragmatism conforms to his belief in the progressive success of the American experiment; it is consistent with his centrist approach to policy making and deliberative decision making. (See Chapter 3.) It is also consistent with his success in adapting to new environments and situations and his political goals of finding consensus among varying perspectives and beliefs.

On the other hand, Obama's pragmatic approach conflicts to some extent with the confident manner in which he arrives at policy judgments. If the policy he formulates is the best antidote to the problems at hand, why weaken it through compromise? Obama's response would likely be that compromise is the price constitutional systems, which divide power, must pay to govern effectively. Compromise is the cost of doing business in a democracy, in which it is important not only to find common ground but to build necessary public support for policy solutions.

But amid his pragmatic and progressive outlook, Obama displays a conservative manner. The esteem he holds for family, community, and country and for roots, cultures, and their traditions makes him seem more like Edmund Burke than John Locke. His political realism also constrains the conversion of his progressive beliefs into liberal public policy. He seems more comfortable in the middle than at the policy extremes; more comfortable on Main Street than any other street (except perhaps the road to the White House). His frequent references to Main Street reinforce the down-to-earth, I-understand-what-you-are-going-through message he wishes to convey.

Obama disdains labels. Despite his liberal voting record as a U.S. senator from Illinois and his government-based initiatives to stimulate the economy, expand health care coverage, and protect the environment, he does not see himself as a liberal ideologue. Far from it, he dislikes all types of 'true believers'. In his writings and speeches, he sees them as part of the problem. In *The Audacity of Hope,* he writes, ". . . it's precisely the pursuit of ideological purity, the rigid orthodoxy, and the sheer predictability of our current debate, that keeps us from finding news ways to meet the challenges we face as a country. It's what keeps us locked in "either/or" thinking . . . ,"[50] a refrain he has repeated in speeches and pre- and post-election interviews and reinforced with his bipartisan appeals to Congress and the American people.

... what we've also seen in these last months is the same partisan spec-
tacle that only hardens the disdain many Americans have towards their
own government. Instead of honest debate, we've seen scare tactics.
Some have dug into unyielding ideological camps that offer no hope of
compromise. Too many have used this as an opportunity to score short-
term political points, even if it robs the country of our opportunity to
solve a long-term challenge. And out of this blizzard of charges and
counter-charges, confusion has reigned.[51]

"It is very hard for us to have a common sense, non-ideological conversation about how we're going to deal with our energy problems,"[52] he told
journalist George Stephanopoulos. To David Mark, he said,

> ... the problem is, when we start breaking down into conservative and
> liberal, and we've got a bunch of set predispositions, whether it's on gun
> control, or it's on health care. . . . The old categories don't work, and
> they're preventing us from solving them (sic) problems.[53]

From a political perspective, Obama's unhappiness with ideologues is
their intellectual stubbornness, their mindset that impedes deliberative
policy making. Ideologues begin with a set of assumptions, use a structured
thought process to apply them, and are more concerned with internal consistency than resolving complex policy disputes. They would rather be
"right" than compromise.

From a psychological perspective, ideologues are too self-imposing, too
confident in the correctness of their views, and as a consequence, too resis-
tant to ideas and applications that challenge their underlying assumptions.
For a conciliator, a healer, a bring-us-together kind of guy, such an attitude
is the antithesis of getting along. It is undemocratic in spirit and practice.
And it goes against Obama's common-ground orientation, his belief in a
United States of America.

Obama also objects to an ideological perspective because it detracts
from civility and contributes to mistrust of others' motives, values, and
interests. During his campaign and presidency, he bemoaned the disagreeable state of American politics: "[W]e can't seem to have disagreements
without being disagreeable."[54]

Nonetheless, his humanistic values and equalitarian goals suggest a liberal policy orientation that explains his liberal voting record in the Senate
and his activist agenda in his first two years as president. Obama thinks of

himself as open-minded, reasonable, and flexible, terms that he does not associate with ideologues of the right or the left. He also perceives himself to be more moderate and centrist than do his critics. It is likely that the political environment following the 2010 midterm elections will force him to pursue a policy agenda that is more incremental than innovative and more stabilizing than redistributive.

Summary

Obama's self-description in a 2006 interview with Jodi Enda, published in *The American Prospect,* summarizes his contemporary policy orientation and political beliefs:

> . . . the way I would describe myself is I think that my values are deeply rooted in the progressive tradition, the values of equal opportunity, civil rights, fighting for working families, a foreign policy that is mindful of human rights, a strong belief in civil liberties, wanting to be a good steward for the environment, a sense that the government has an important role to play, that opportunity is open to all people and that the powerful don't trample on the less powerful . . .[55]

Obama believes in the possibility of transformational leadership but also subscribes to the principles of participatory democracy and the pragmatism of contemporary politics. He perceives government as having an obligation to help people in need, but he is aware of the skepticism with which Americans view new and costly national government programs. He supports the free enterprise system but also favors a stronger regulatory role for government, particularly in the economic arena. He is sensitive to discriminatory practices but also believes in the merits of volunteerism, rooted communities, religious groups, and social networks. He lauds the American political tradition but also acknowledges the unfairness, inequities, and injustices that that tradition produced and protected over the years.

Obama sees participatory democracy based on common interests and values as the answer to the politics of special interests and bipartisanship as the antidote to partisan political rhetoric and actions. He advocates a foreign policy based on diplomacy and mutual respect, a strong military establishment, and continued vigilance in the prevention of terrorism. He is a family man who believes in the sanctity of marriage but also acknowledges the rights and duties of individuals in nontraditional familial relationships. He is proud of American accomplishments but also mindful of the need for continuing economic and social change. And he knows from his experience as president that such change will not come easily, quickly, or quietly. There will be opposition from people who benefit from existing conditions, perceive change as harmful to their interests, or simply fear it or believe it is unnecessary.

Achieving these diverse and often competing policy objectives requires persuasion and skill. He uses high sounding rhetoric combined with sophisticated communication techniques to spread the message, engage the populace, and pressure policy makers. So long as he can claim the high ground, he is amenable to compromise. He is adamant about the priorities that accord with his vision but flexible on the details of the policy itself.

For Obama, bipartisanship is both a means and an end. It is a way to build an issue-based majority in a manner that is consistent with his common interests and common-ground vision of how democratic societies should operate. It is also consistent with his need to be a conciliator, to bring diverse communities together, and with the public image he wishes to project as a unifier capable of rising above petty partisan politics and appealing to the common aspirations of the American people.

Thus, for Obama, goals take precedence over policy specifics; bipartisanship reconciles a philosopher–king orientation within a belief in participatory democracy; and pragmatism becomes an operational approach for decision making as well as a reality check for a person with elitist tendencies, a president who fears being encased in a bubble, and a politician desirous of reelection by a heterogeneous electorate.

NOTES

1. Barack Obama, *The Audacity of Hope* (New York: Crown, 2006), 55.
2. Ibid.
3. Ibid., 31. Like Ronald Reagan, Obama was able to lift public spirits in the short run following his election, but he has not been able to persuade Americans to discard their conservative policy orientation or their suspicion of government, particularly the national government in Washington.
4. Barack Obama, "Inaugural Address," January 20, 2009, www.whitehouse.gov.

5. Barack Obama, "Keynote Address at the 2004 Democratic National Convention," July 27, 2004, www.barackobama.com/2004/07/27/keynote_address_at_the_2004_de.php.

6. Barack Obama, "A More Perfect Union," March 18, 2008, www.reobama.com/SpeechesMarch1808.htm.

7. Obama, "Inaugural Address."

8. Barack Obama, "Press Conference," February 8, 2009, www.whitehouse.gov.

9. Barack Obama, "Commencement Address at Notre Dame University," South Bend, Indiana, May 17, 2009, www.whitehouse.gov.

10. Barack Obama, "Address at Cairo University," June 4, 2009, www.whitehouse.gov.

11. Gallup Poll, "Topics A–Z: Satisfaction with the United States," www.gallup.com/poll/1669/General-Mood-Country.aspx; "Topics A–Z: Consumer Views of the Economy," www.gallup.com/poll/1609/Consummer-Views-Economy.aspx.

12. Obama, *Audacity,* 207.

13. Cathleen Falsani, "Transcript of 2004 Obama Interview," *Christianity Today,* May 27, 2008, http://blog.christianitytoday.com/ctpolitics/2008/11/obamas_fascinat.html.

14. In his races for state legislature, Obama had always done better among the liberal white population in the mixed racial community of Hyde Park than among African Americans concentrated in another part of his state senate district.

15. Obama, *Audacity,* 202.

16. Mayhill Fowler, "Obama: No Surprise That Hard-Pressed Pennsylvanians Turn Bitter," *Huffington Post,* April 11, 2008, www.huffingtonpost.com/mayhill-fowler/obama-no-surprise-that-ha_b_96188.html.

17. Obama, *Audacity,* 207.

18. Cathleen Falsani, "Obama: I Have a Deep Faith," *Chicago Sun-Times,* April 5, 2004, blog.beliefnet.com/stevenwaldman/2008/11/obamas-interview-with-cathleen.html.

19. Falsani, "2004 Obama Interview."

20. Falsani, "I Have a Deep Faith."

21. Obama, *Audacity,* 224.

22. Ibid., 221.

23. Sarah Pulliam and Ted Olsen, "Q & A: Barack Obama," *Christianity Today,* June 2, 2008, www.ctlibrary.com/ct/2008/januaryweb-only/104-32.0.html.

24. Falsani, "I Have a Deep Faith."

25. Falsani, "2004 Obama Interview."

26. Obama, *Audacity,* 220.

27. David Brody, "Obama to CBN News: We're No Longer Just a Christian Nation," *Christian Broadcast Network,* July 2007, http://www.cbn.com/CBNnews/204016.aspx.

28. Falsani, "I Have a Deep Faith."

29. Obama, *Audacity,* 212.
30. Ibid., 211.
31. Jodi Kantor, "Teaching Law, Testing Ideas, Obama Stood Slightly Apart," *New York Times,* July 30, 2008, www.nytimes.com/2008/07/30/us/politics/30law .html?pagewanted=all.
32. Obama, *Audacity,* 52.
33. Ibid.
34. Ibid., 40.
35. "Transcript: Obama Full Interview with NPR," *National Public Radio,* June 1, 2009, www.npr.org/templates/story/story.php?storyId=104806528.
36. Obama, *Audacity,* 92.
37. Obama, "A More Perfect Union."
38. Fareed Zakaria, "CNN's Global Public Square," CNN, July 13, 2008, www .cnn.com/CNN/Programs/fareed.zakaria.gps.
39. Barack Obama, "Address to a Joint Session of Congress," September 9, 2009, www.whitehouse.gov.
40. Obama, *Audacity,* 159.
41. Obama, "Address to a Joint Session," September 9, 2009.
42. This belief led to his support of enhanced regulations and increased government monitoring for banks, credit card companies, and the investment community, for protecting the environment and getting those who damage it to pay to clean it up (British Petroleum for the oil spill in the Gulf of Mexico), and for improving medical research by expanding stem cell research, discouraging children from smoking, and extending health care insurance to all who want it.
43. "Part of the change in attitudes that I want to see here in Washington and all across the country is a belief that it is not acceptable for children and families to be without a roof over their heads in a country as wealthy as ours." Barack Obama, "Address to a Joint Session of Congress," February 24, 2009, www .whitehouse.gov.
44. David Remnick, *The Bridge* (New York: Knopf, 2010), 448.
45. Barack Obama, "Acceptance Speech at the Democratic National Convention," August 28, 2008, www.nytimes.com/2008/08/28/us/politics/28text-obama .html.
46. Obama, "Press Conference," February 9, 2009.
47. Obama, "Remarks by the President After Briefing on BP Oil Spill," May 28, 2010, www.whitehouse.gov/the-press-office/remarks-president-after-brief ing-bp-oil-spill.
48. John Harwood, "Interview on CNBC," January 7, 2009, www.nytimes .com/2009/01/08/us/politics/08obama.html.
49. E. J. Dionne, "Obama Interview Transcript," *Washington Post,* February 17, 2009, voices.washingtonpost.com/postpartisan/2009/02/obama_interview_ transcript.html.

50. Obama, *Audacity,* 40.
51. Obama, "Address to a Joint Session," September 9, 2009.
52. George Stephanopoulos, "Transcript of Obama Interview," *ABC This Week,* January 11, 2009, http://abcnews.go.com/ThisWeek/Economy/story?id=6618199&page=2.
53. David Mark, "Obama Interview," *Politico,* February 11, 2008.
54. Stephanopoulos, "Obama Interview."
55. Jodi Enda, "Great Expectations," *American Prospect,* January 16, 2006, www.prospect.org/cs/articles?articleId=10828.

3

OPERATING STYLE

"You've got to make decisions based on information and not emotions."

— Obama in Joel Achenbach, "In His Slow Decision-Making, Obama Goes with Head, Not Gut"[*]

"The things that for me work day to day become that much more important in a crisis: being able to pull together the best people and have them work as a team; insisting on analytical rigor in evaluating the nature of the problem; making sure that dissenting voices are heard and that a range of options are explored; being willing to make a decision after having looked at all the options, and then insisting on good execution as well as timely feedback, so that [if] you have to correct the decision that you make, that you are able to do so in time; being able to stay calm and steady when the stakes are high."

— Obama in Kenneth T. Walsh, "Exclusive Interview: Obama 'Never 100 Percent Certain' "[*]

"I don't get too high when I'm high and I don't get too low when I am low."

— Obama, "Transcript: Obama on 'FNS' "[*]

---

[*]Joel Achenbach, "In His Slow Decision-Making, Obama Goes with Head, Not Gut," *Washington Post*, November 25, 2009.

[*]Kenneth T. Walsh, "Exclusive Interview: Obama 'Never 100 Percent Certain,'" *U.S. News & World Report*, October 27, 2009.

[*]"Transcript: Barack Obama on 'FNS'" Fox News, April 27, 2008, www.foxnews.com/story/0,2933,352785,00.html.

Barack Obama is obviously a very intelligent man. He learns easily and quickly. Confident of his ability to analyze complex issues and make good judgments, Obama is a rational decision maker. He is thorough, dispassionate, and careful; energetic, even-tempered, and consensus oriented; he strives for the practical, not the theoretical. He likes to please, and profits politically and personally from doing so.

He is comfortable in his own skin, about his own beliefs, and with his ability to adjust to new and different circumstances and environments. As noted in Chapter 1, his struggle for identity provided him with confidence to understand, appreciate, and operate successfully in different social and political environments. It also gave him a foundation on which to stand and from which to comprehend policy issues. He has a broad and flexible mindset to tackle contemporary issues.

Obama is not without traits that can adversely affect his decision making on public policy issues and the implementation of that policy, however. He is risk adverse, extremely cautious, and can be slow to rush to judgment. Despite his claim that his life experience qualifies him to understand and appreciate the plight of a diverse community, he often appears distant and remote from everyday folks. He reluctantly admits mistakes, as do most politicians. Moreover, his propensity to look for common ground clashes with the imagery he has projected and the campaign promises he made to transform the political environment and change public policy.

Cognition

Obama is a deep thinker with broad and flexible frames of reference. He reacts against the intellectual shortcuts that a consistent ideological perspective provides and instead approaches issues pragmatically, using popularist language to justify his goals and build public support for them. Although his upbringing sensitizes him to the plight of minorities in a democratic polity, one in which economic advantage is reinforced by political power, his public policy thinking has also been shaped by the values he places on community, heritage, custom—values that should result in more conservative policy decisions.

Obama's intellectuality, particularly his legal training, undergraduate education in political philosophy, and his training in legal reasoning, affects how he thinks. Rigor, logic, and rationality guide his thought processes. He tends to keep whatever emotions he feels well buried. He does not believe that emotions should affect policy judgments. "You've got to make decisions based on information and not emotions," he has stated.[1]

Confident of his synthetic and analytic skills, Obama reads vociferously: books, briefing papers, newspapers, personal letters and e-mails, usually until the late hours of the evening. Although he deals with and enjoys the challenge of theoretical questions and abstract judgments, his penchant is to stay in touch with what's real and what directly affects people's lives. He keeps his focus on the doable, not the optimal. He describes himself (with little modesty) as ". . . a practical person, somebody who, I think can cut through some very complicated problems and figure out the right course of action."[2]

Obama thinks when he writes. His two books and the countless hours he spent writing them enabled him to work through his identity issues as well as the broader policy concerns he discussed in the campaign and has confronted as president. His speech on race relations following the Jeremiah Wright controversy was written primarily by Obama himself, alone in a hotel room over a period of 48 hours. As president, he continues to outline and edit his speeches, but with the exception of his Inaugural address and one or two other major speeches, he has not had time to write them himself; however, he works closely with Jon Favreau, his principal campaign and White House speech writer, and others who have worked with him in the past.

Obama is not prone to make rash judgments, except in instances in which his political ambitions get in the way of a slower, more cautious and calculating decisional process. One of the hasty decisions he made was his challenge to Rep. Bobby Rush in the 2000 congressional primaries in Illinois, a challenge in which Obama was decisively defeated; another instinctive decision was to give the speech on race during the campaign. Of that speech, he said,

> My gut was telling me that this was a teachable moment and that if I tried to do the usual political damage control instead of talking to the American people like an adult . . . I would not only be doing damage to the campaign but missing an important opportunity for leadership.[3]

But gut decisions tend to be the exception, not the rule, for Obama. He believes that good judgment requires a lot of information from a variety of sources and points of view, plus the time and mindset to sort them all out and make a quality decision. He is confident of his judgments that have resulted from a deliberative decision-making process, so much so that he tends to stick with them even when popular opinion shifts, critics question his decision, or short-term results are disappointing. Careful not to let peripheral changes in the environment overturn previously considered judgments, Obama sees persistence as one of his most redeeming characteristics.

When it came to light that the insurance giant, AIG—a company that had borrowed $174 billion from the federal government to survive—gave bonuses to its executives, Obama was asked why he took several days to react publicly. He snapped, "It took us a couple of days because I like to know what I'm talking about before I speak."[4] The press viewed his response as an indication of annoyance for a hostile question that diverted him from the subject he wanted to discuss.

Obama's response, however, was consistent with his desire to consider a variety of information and advice before deciding on a course of action. It was also consistent with his aversion to emotionally laden reactions. As a well-schooled lawyer and practitioner, Obama prides himself on the clarity, precision, and logic of his thinking. Although criticized for hesitancy and indecision before ordering 30,000 additional troops to Afghanistan and during the first few weeks of the large Gulf oil spill, Obama did not rush to judgment. That's not his style.

In short, Obama's cognitive process is a product of his legal training, his nonideological mindset, and his integrative orientation. He tends to think broadly and deeply. Such thinking requires the capacity to synthesize and analyze a great deal of information in a careful, logical, and incisive manner to arrive at judgments that meet the tests of rigor, rationality, and practicality.

Obama's pragmatism keeps him close to political realities. He seeks empirical evidence. His is a fact-based decisional process with collective deliberation at its core. The process of deliberation enlarges the information base, helps clarify the options, and improves support for the final judgment. Building this support among policy experts, a consensus if possible, seems as important to Obama as the substance of the decision itself.

Decision Making

As noted previously, Obama's style is to assemble policy experts, encourage a debate among them, and arrive at a collective judgment. He listens, asks questions, gains perspectives, and then armed with information, he tries to fashion a consensus-based decision. He does not want to be blindsided, hence the need for alternative perspectives and recommendations.

He also likes "to keep the process crisp."[5] Nonetheless, White House policy sessions during his first years in office have tended to last longer than originally planned, for which the president usually apologizes to those present and participating.[6] Obama does not cut corners in making major policy decisions.

In an interview with Kenneth T. Walsh of *U.S. News & World Report,* posted on October 27, 2009, the president said,

> The things that for me work day to day become that much more important in a crisis: being able to pull together the best people and have them work as a team; insisting on analytical rigor in evaluating the nature of the problem; making sure that dissenting voices are heard and that a range of options are explored; being willing to make a decision after having looked at all the options, and then insisting on good execution as well as timely feedback, so that [if] you have to correct the decision that you make, that you are able to do so in time; being able to stay calm and steady when the stakes are high . . . the decisions are tough and the consequences of action are most weighty.[7]

Before the election, Obama's advisers marveled at his thoughtfulness, incisiveness, and rigor in making policy judgments. According to David Axelrod, his chief political strategist:

> He's very methodical in how he evaluates decisions. He asks a series of questions. He'll engage you in dialogue on the options. And then he'll make a decision. And he doesn't look back at that decision.[8]

Christopher Lu, Obama's legislative aide in the Senate and now a White House staffer noted, "He wanted us to argue it out in front of him, and he probed each side's arguments and asked hypotheticals, almost like a judge."[9] Abner Mikva, former representative from Illinois and federal judge, a mentor to the young Obama in Chicago, put it this way:

> I have never seen anybody in the political arena who can be as deliberate and cool as he is on decisions. In all the years I've known him, I've never seen him emotionally angry. I'm sure he's been—. . . I could tell he was upset at times, but the emotions never went into the decisional process.[10]

David Plouffe, Obama's 2008 campaign manager, described the candidate's decision-making process in choosing a vice president as "methodical, calm, and purposeful," adding ". . . I could envision this behavior and approach translating very well to the Oval Office, where steadiness and rigorous thought and questioning would serve him and the country well."[11]

The confidence that Obama displays in his decision making stems from his success in coping with new environments, his academic and professional achievements, and his rabid rise to positions of increasing power. Self-reliant at an early age, he had to learn to hang tough, stand up for what he wanted, make his own decisions, and have faith in them.

Obama becomes an educator when he writes, speaks, and decides. As a law professor, he encouraged his students to examine their own biases and orientations, base their arguments on sound empirical data, and evaluate the impact of judicial arguments and decisions on contemporary society. He obviously sees argumentation and collective analysis as important components of the learning process.

He enjoys the intellectual challenge of public policy decisions. That challenge enables him to demonstrate his intellectual skills among experts, to show off his knowledge. He occasionally displays impatience when the discussion becomes too basic.[12] In his daily meetings with his economic advisers, *Wall Street Journal* reporters Neil King Jr. and Jonathan Weisman write,

> In the sessions, according to those who attend, the president sometimes chafes at his advisers' limitations, quizzing them on points raised by critics or asking them to do justice to a view other than their own. At times he quotes from letters sent to the White House to counter a stance taken by his team."[13]

This "show off" quality is another dimension of Obama's need to make others aware of his knowledge and his capability of using it effectively. For Obama, showing off his smarts is part of his mystique. The knowledge he displays reinforces confidence that people have in his judgment. That confidence, however, has angered some of his critics, many of whom see him as glib, even condescending, overly academic, and out of touch with real people and their real feelings. This perception has contributed to the charge of elitism directed at Obama during the 2008 presidential campaign and subsequently in the White House.

The strengths of the president's decision-making style are its wide scope and deep analysis. Unlike the "group think" allegations directed at George W. Bush's policy advisers, particularly with respect to the war in Iraq, Obama desires diverse policy advice. He prefers argumentation in the beginning, but seeks consensus at the end.

Obama's decision making has its shortcomings, however. The process can be slow and requires a large commitment of the president's time and energy as well as that of others highly placed in the White House and executive branch hierarchy. As noted earlier in this chapter, Obama's decision making style is to factor out emotions as much as possible. Yet, public emotions gain press visibility, affect evaluations of government, and thus have political consequences. Intensity matters in politics.

Obama's preferred mode of decision making devalues instinct, political or otherwise, even though those types of reactions may combine experience, emotion, and desire, all of which potentially affect behavior. To downplay unconscious feelings because they cannot be articulated or defended rationally is to exclude an important dimension of reality, which in turn may affect the outcome or impact of the policy judgment.

Finally, Obama's decision making conflicts with the democratic goal of transparency in government. For the process to work, participants must be free to express opinions that may be unpopular and do so in ways that may not conform to accepted standards of public discourse. Subjecting White House decision making to immediate and on-going public scrutiny would inhibit discussion and skew decisions toward short-term outcomes rather than those that take a longer, more nuanced view of policy and the public interest.

No process is perfect. Different situations demand differing decisional criteria and often different processes to arrive at them. Some decisions need to be made quickly, some tentatively, and/or privately; others are affected by the time frame of elections, the resources available to the president, or the cycle for exercising presidential power. Some decisions will be affected by the public mood, the partisan political climate, or international pressures and national interests.

Nonetheless, most presidential scholars agree that the process of decision making must be consistent with the president's style, enhance his ability to make a sound policy or political judgment, and also contribute to the implementation of that judgment by the president, his aides, or others over whom he exercises some authority.[14]

Organization

Obama is an organization man. Although he demonstrated managerial skills on the streets of Chicago as a community organizer and in the campaigns he ran for Senate and president, his interest lies more in solving public policy issues, exercising political leadership, and communicating his beliefs and judgments than in the day-to-day operations. During the election, he was content to leave the "nuts and bolts" of running a campaign to his senior staff, although he did participate in an evening conference call that focused more on strategies, tactics, and message than on budget and management concerns.[15] He gave his campaign manager, Plouffe, considerable flexibility in hiring staff, directing operations, and overseeing the operation of the campaign.

There was very little staff turnover during the election in large part because the staff believed in Obama, willingly sacrificed for him, and the campaign was successful. Few people wish to leave a winning team. Obama's presidential campaign followed the strategic plan designed at the beginning by his principal advisers, even in the face of some disappointing results (New Hampshire and Pennsylvania), unanticipated events (the release of the Reverend Wright's sermons and the temporary suspension of John McCain's presidential campaign during the financial crisis, and an occasional slip of the tongue by Obama), and the ups and downs of the polls, another illustration of the confidence Obama places in a well-considered and thought-out judgment.

Mistakes were made, but not many. Obama was careful not to assign blame. His style with his campaign staff was to commiserate after disappointments and build morale. He rarely lost his temper, although he could become testy when tired.

During the campaign, Obama, a candidate with limited executive experience, downplayed the importance of managerial skills for a president. In a January 14, 2008, interview with the editorial board of the *Reno Gazette-Journal,* he was quoted as saying,

> I'm not an operating officer. Some in this debate around experience seem to think the job of the president is to go in and run some bureaucracy. Well, that's not my job. My job is to set a vision of "Here's where the bureaucracy needs to go."[16]

In the Democratic debate preceding the Nevada caucus, he stated, probably half in jest:

> My desk and my office doesn't look good. I've got to have somebody around me who is keeping track of that stuff. And that's not trivial; I need to have good people in place who can make sure that systems run.

That's what I've always done, that what's why we run not only a good campaign, but a good U.S. Senate office.[17]

In creating a White House organization and appointing a staff, Obama followed the practice of most newly elected presidents, recruiting staff whose loyalty, work ethic, and in the case of former Clinton aides, experience had been successfully demonstrated in electoral campaigns, Congress, or previous White Houses. Somewhat ironically, Obama has benefited from the "insider" expertise that he disparaged during his nomination and general election campaigns.

On the advice of former chiefs of staff, he appointed his top White House aides first, beginning with his chief of staff, Rahm Emanuel, and followed by his principal economic, national security, and domestic advisers. His White House was designed to enhance Obama's focus on transforming policy and providing leadership in his first two years in office. It was also designed to take advantage of the momentum generated by a historic election, the Democrat's large congressional majority, and the policy crises he faced to build and maintain political support for his legislative priorities.

Eight policy czars were initially appointed to reinforce Obama's emphasis on policy making. Their job was to coordinate executive branch advice, participate in decision-making sessions, and act as administrative spokespersons.[18] They had small staffs, few administrative responsibilities, and no independent budgets. The czars were people with considerable policy expertise who could be expected to provide the president with a full range of information and advice.

Obamas's White House and Cabinet staffing was influenced by Doris Kearns Goodwin's book on Lincoln, *Team of Rivals*.[19] Obama admired Lincoln, read the book, and met with the author to learn more about the Lincoln experience.[20] He liked the idea of generating internal debate within his administration and arriving at a consensus that a diverse group of advisers could support. It was consistent with Obama's preference for deliberative decision making and contrasted sharply with the group-think mentality for which his predecessor had been criticized. Having knowledgeable policy experts discuss complex issues also supplemented Obama's own lack of experience in certain policy areas.

With the exception of the inner cabinet departments (State, Defense, Treasury, and Justice), cabinet secretaries were distanced from the center of power in the White House. The president was content, at least at the outset

President Obama meets with cabinet on June 22, 2010.

of his administration, to let his secretaries run their own departments, occasionally respond to policy issues in their own areas of responsibility, and serve as conduits to the groups and interests that made up their departmental clientele. Policy issues that cut across departmental lines were to be coordinated from the White House and budget matters from the Office of Management and Budget.

As president, Obama has relied primarily on White House aides to staff his multiple roles, as do most presidents. Aides scheduled his day, prepared informational briefs, drafted his speeches, and coordinated on-going communications that supported the public dimension of his presidency. Obama enjoys public attention; he uses speech and ceremony to enhance his leadership image, much as Ronald Reagan did. Obama's presidency has been a constant campaign for his policy agenda, job approval, and the projection of a strong leadership image.

Communication

For Obama, words can have power and have given him power, particularly during his 2008 presidential campaign. They provided the spark that ignited and expanded his broad following during his presidential campaign, kept his war chests filled, brought large crowds to his rallies, and supplied his organization with thousands of volunteers. Initially, as president, his words signaling policy change were well received abroad, helped sustain his leadership image, and contributed to favorable job performance ratings. Words initially helped him explain the economic measures he was taking to stimulate the economy and redeem his campaign promises on energy, the environment, and health care reform, but over time seemed empty in the absence of discernible changes to conditions most Americans viewed as undesirable.

Although his has been a very public presidency, Obama's communications have not produced the kind of public response they did during his nomination and general election campaign. As a candidate he was inspirational, promising change, giving hope, and conveying confidence that with public support he would be successful. As president he has been more subdued, matter-of-fact, professorial, and at times defensive. He has also been less focused, given the multiple responsibilities he has, issues he has faced, and constituencies he must address.

As a person and communicator, Obama is extremely disciplined. He is cautious with his words, careful not to err by being too verbose or flippant, a tendency he has noted in himself.[21] During his campaign, he kept reporters at a distance, aware that an ad-lib comment, emotional response, or poorly chosen words could cause considerable damage. Nonetheless, he did make a few careless remarks that became points of contention during his campaign and after he became president.

Obama's use of the term "bitter" to describe folks in small-town America and his pledge to meet with leaders of countries, friend or foe, without preconditions are two examples in which the meaning of his words had to be clarified, and in the case of the word "bitter," admitted to be inappropriate.[22]

Obama also had to apologize to Nancy Reagan for a flippant comment he made about her in a press conference. When asked if he had spoken with any ex-presidents since his election, Obama replied that he had spoken with "all living ex-presidents," adding "I didn't want to get into a Nancy Reagan thing about, you know, doing any séances."[23]

In an interview with Jay Leno after becoming president, he noted his bowling score of 129, adding, "It's like—it was like Special Olympics, or something."[24] His aides, immediately recognized the insensitivity of his comment and suggested that he telephone Eunice Shriver, who along with her husband, R. Sargent Shriver, had championed such events for disabled people. Obama made the call as well as one to Sen. Ted Kennedy.

As a candidate, he participated in more than twenty-four debates with his political opponents; as president he held three televised press conferences in his first 100 days of office, and has had numerous one-on-one interviews. The most remarkable aspects of these mostly nonscripted appearances is the consistency he displayed in words and thoughts and his willingness again and again to explain his beliefs. He rarely responds angrily to interviewers.

One occasion in which he did display anger occurred during the campaign when he was accused on misrepresenting his vote in the Illinois state legislature on a bill called the Born Alive Infant Protection Act by National Right to Life committee. He snapped,

> . . . they have not been telling the truth. And I hate to say that people are lying, but here's a situation where folks are lying. So for people to suggest that I and the Illinois Medical society . . . were somehow in favor of withholding life saving support from an infant born alive is ridiculous. It defies commonsense and it defies imagination and for people to keep on pushing this it's offensive and it's an example of the kind of politics that we have to get beyond.[25]

Although Obama has a way with words, he does use and re-use certain expressions. "You know" is one of his standard terms, an expression that suggests the obvious nature of the information he is about to present. "Well, look" is another phrase that reappears frequently in his oral responses to questions. At times, both expressions seem to suggest some impatience, but they are repeated so matter of factly that listeners would probably not take umbrage.

His campaign and presidential interviews are strewn with "I think." His emphasis here seems to be on the "I," stipulating that what he is presenting is a personal opinion. It sets his opinion apart from others and gives him credit for it. The use of the word "think" may also at some unconscious level demonstrate his preference for rational and logical thought processes rather than instinctive reactions that he associates more with emotions. Here's an example from an interview with David Leonhardt, published in the *New York Times Magazine,* April 28, 2009:

> *I think* a healthy economy is going to have a broad mix of jobs, and there has to be a place for somebody with terrific mechanical aptitude who can perform highly skills tasks with his hands, . . . And *I don't think* that those jobs should vanish. *I do think* that they will constitute a smaller percentage of the overall economy.[26]

Obama can be his own best publicist. He rarely loses opportunities to teach others, and criticized George W. Bush for not taking advantage of the president's bully pulpit to educate the American people. In an interview with *The New Yorker's* David Remnick, conducted well before the 2008 election, Obama said,

. . . the power of the presidency that I don't see used enough [is] the capacity to explain to the American people in very prosaic, straightforward terms: here are the choices we have . . . the biggest problem we have in our politics . . . is to lie about the choices that have to be made.[27]

He made the same point in an interview with Steve Kroft on CBS News program *60 Minutes*.

. . . one of the things that I do think is important is to be able to explain to the American people what you're doing, and why you're doing it. That is something that I think every great president has been able to do from FDR to Lincoln to John Kennedy to Eisenhower.[28]

Obama referred to this learning experience as an important reason for deciding to give his speech on race during the campaign. He stated to *Newsweek*'s Jon Meacham:

. . . one of the things I've actually been encouraged by and I learned during the campaign was the American people, I think, not only have a toleration but also a hunger for explanation and complexity, and a willingness to acknowledge hard problems. I think one of the biggest mistakes that is made in Washington is this notion you have to dumb things down for the public.[29]

Obama regarded the press and public reaction to his comment on the incident involving the arrest of Harvard professor Henry Gates as one of those "teachable moments" and his acceptance of the Nobel peace prize as another.[30]

Words are powerful not only because of these opportunities to educate but also because they allow Obama to demonstrate his knowledge, intelligence, and command of the subject matter, which in turn generates confidence that he knows what he is talking about. Obama has certainly benefited from the comparison with his immediate predecessor's intellectual and communicative skills.

Rhetoric is also a critical component of Obama's belief in the importance of deliberation in a representative government. A proponent of participatory democracy, Obama believes that informed debate not only results in better judgments being made but it also generates a more civil tone. Civility, in turn, contributes to compromise, which is consistent with Obama's conciliator style of personal interaction as well as the leadership imagery he wishes to project.

In short, words allow Obama to shine, to demonstrate his intelligence, his thoughtfulness, and occasionally his wit. From a psychological perspective, Obama has gotten positive feedback and much adulation from his ability to inspire and to educate. The importance he attaches to public discourse also helps explain his admiration for the communicative skills of Ronald Reagan and to the emphasis his presidential campaign placed on developing new communication technologies to reach a broader cross-section of voters.

Obama ran a bottom-up campaign that encouraged social networking. Campaign aides found the Internet to be a quick and cheap way to reach out, particularly to younger Americans. His advisers subsequently established a White House blog and have encouraged communication from everyday folks. As president-elect, Obama fought to keep his Black-Berry. He claimed it was an instrument in which he could use to get out of the White House bubble, the protective environment in which presidents are forced to live.[31] Most days, he reads ten of the many letters and e-mails received daily at the White House. Occasionally he answers them personally.

In choosing his words, he usually errs on the side of caution. He is careful, confident, and composed. Obama exercises self-discipline for political as well as personal reasons. The political reasons are obvious. Succeeding in the electoral arena as a minority candidate requires rhetoric and behavior that conforms to the majority's political and cultural perspective, its social mores and language patterns, rather than to the minority's distinctive character, and manner of speaking.

Obama's political needs are consistent with the leadership image he tries to project, the policy goals he wants to achieve, and an upbeat public appeal he desires to make. His personal needs relate to adaptation and acceptance. Obama is a man who needs to fit in and be seen in a positive light by people with whom he is engaged. Thus the defeat his party suffered in the 2010 midterm elections must have taken a personal toll on Obama, who blamed himself for his communication failures as president and promised to do better.

Conciliation

Obama preaches the politics of reconciliation. His bring-us-together attitude and a common-ground appeal is his answer to the divisions generated by a diverse society. It is also an effective message for a minority candidate who wants to demonstrate his mainstream American values and beliefs.

For Obama, conciliation has become a personal philosophy as well as a skills' set, a means and an end. Consistent with his life experience of how to get along amid diversity, national conciliation was an effective campaign message to voters tired of decades of ideologically driven partisanship, special-interests politics, and divisive policy issues, as well as a strategy for governing in a constitutional system that divides power and encourages a polarized party system.

As an end, conciliation is a way to get along in a heterogeneous society. It is consistent with Obama's belief in the merits of an ordered society governed by the rule of law and his penchant for seeking change within the system rather than outside of it. It is also in keeping with his belief that participation in public policy judgments increases legitimacy and support for those policy judgments.

A conciliatory attitude enabled Obama to demonstrate attributes in the 2008 nomination process and general election that distinguished him from political opponents as well as his presidential predecessor: an even temperament, level headedness, pragmatism, and flexibility.

For Obama, the practice of conciliatory politics has brought mixed results. He has trouble bridging the partisan divide successfully on a regular basis, and he has not been able to change public perceptions and attitudes about governing. Although he has been able to achieve legislative compromises among Democrats and for the most part, maintain a united front within his administration, he has not achieved the national unity he preached and promised during his presidential campaign. The political, social, and economic divisions within the country and the suspicions they generated have been deeper and more resilient to change than Obama's campaign oratory suggested. The economic recession and slow recovery have exacerbated these divisions and undermined Obama's bipartisan appeal.

Summary

Style is how a person goes about doing work and relating to others. It is developed from self-perceived successes and failures in performing functions critical to achieving personal and professional goals. It is a pattern of performance that becomes unconscious over time, to which people adhere so long as it produces the desired results.

To look authentic, style has to be consistent with a person's personality, specifically with personal needs that require fulfillment and deficiencies, real or imagined, that must be hidden so as not to impede the achievement of one's goals. Some people fear that they will be found out, that others will see them for what they really are, not for how they would like to be seen. In this sense, style is like clothes; it portrays a desirable image, what we would like people to see.

Obama's presidential style stems from his success in college and law school and as a law school professor, candidate for public office, state and national legislator, and now as president. One component of that style is the way he thinks, a component that relates to his educational experience, legal training, and practice in making policy judgments as candidate and legislator, and as president.

Despite his idealistic campaign rhetoric in 2008, Obama is a realist. Thus his legal arguments, constitutional interpretations, and policy judgments need to be grounded in the practical, what's possible, not necessarily the theoretical and certainly not the ideological. Confident of his ability to synthesize and analyze complex problems, Obama is also a generalist. Without study, he does not come to policy-oriented decisions with the detailed knowledge of an expert, hence his need to assemble people with that knowledge and then explore their assumptions and assess their policy recommendations.

Obama is confident in judgments made in accordance with a deliberative, decision-making style. He avoids spur-of-the-moment decisions. The confidence he has in his judgment inclines him to stick with his decisions unless and until new information suggests otherwise. His pragmatism, however, requires frequent reality checks.

Obama's White House was designed to serve his decisional needs, policy-making priorities, and leadership style. The initial structure was heavily oriented toward providing the information and coordination to achieve a consensus within the administration on the policy issues he promised to address during his 2007–2008 presidential campaign. Eight policy-making offices were initially established to assess needs, coordinate executive and congressional input, propose recommendations, and debate outcomes, and after the president's decision, to ensure that the policy was executed in accordance with his desires.

An elaborate public relations mechanism was also designed to orchestrate the public dimensions of his presidency, with Obama taking the role of spokesperson, teacher, and persuader. Although he considers rhetoric a source of power for him, one from which he also derives adulation, his public presidency has not been nearly as successful as he hoped and undoubtedly anticipated. For many Americans, there has been a disconnect between his words and policies and the economic improvement people expected.

Obama thrives on the policy challenges, the dialogue with international leaders, and the ceremonial parts of his job. Internal, partisan politics have been rougher than he initially imagined; his bipartisan approach has not reaped the bipartisan support he desired except during the lame duck session of the 111th Congress. He dislikes partisan bickering and people holding uncompromising policy positions, and seems impatient with the pace and sometimes the product of legislative deliberations. He has responded to increasing press and public criticism by tweaking his public manner and making some White House staff adjustments, but he has not altered his decision-making style or reduced the multiple roles he as assumed as president.

Although Obama has occasionally shown impatience, he rarely explodes in anger. He does not demonize his opponents or do anything publicly that would run counter to his conciliator approach and his common-ground goals. His style, however, undercuts the image he has projected as a transformational leader. Tensions among his character, style, and policy goals have also been evident. In the next chapter we explore these tensions and the challenges they pose for him as president.

NOTES

1. Joel Achenbach, "In His Slow Decision-Making, Obama Goes with Head, Not Gut," *Washington Post*, November 25, 2009, www.washingtonpost.com/wp-dyn/content/article/2009/11/24/AR2009112404225.html?hpid=topnews.
2. Steve Kroft, "Interview of Barack Obama on *60 Minutes*," CBS News, September 17, 2008, www.cbsnews.com/story/09/17/60 minutes/main4476095.
3. Joe Klein, "The Full Obama Interview," *Time*, October 23, 2008, http://swamp-land.blogs.time.com/2008/10/23/the_full_obama_interview.
4. Barack Obama, "Presidential News Conference," March 24, 2009, www whitehouse gov
5. Jeff Zeleny and Jim Rutenberg, "A Delegator, Obama Picks When to Take Reins," *New York Times*, June 16, 2008, www.nytimes.com/2008/06/16/us/politics/16manage.html.
6. Neil King Jr. and Jonathan Weisman, "A President as Micromanager: How Much Detail Is Enough?" *Wall Street Journal*, August 12, 2009, http://online.wsj.com/article/SB125003045380123953.html.
7. Kenneth T. Walsh, "Obama Defends Waiting on Afghanistan Decision," *U.S. News & World Report*, October 27, 2009, www.usnews.com/.../articles/2009/10/27/obama-defends-waiting-on-afghanistan-decision.html.

8. Margaret Warner, "Confidence, Openness Mark Obama's Decision Making Style," *News Hour*, September 23, 2008, www.pbs.org/newshour/bb/politics/july-dec08/obamacloseup_09-23.html.

9. Eli Saslow, "A Rising Political Star Adopts a Low-Key Strategy," *Washington Post*, October, 17 2008, A7, www.washingtonpost.com/wp-dyn/content/article/2008/10/16/AR2008101604277.html.

10. Ibid.

11. David Plouffe, *The Audacity to Win* (New York: Viking, 2009), 285.

12. King and Weisman, "President as Micromanager."

13. Ibid.

14. See George C. Edwards III and Stephen J. Wayne, *Presidential Leadership: Politics and Policy Making* (Wadsworth/Cengage Learning, 2010), 229–62; Karen M. Hult and Charles E. Walcott, "Influences on Presidential Decision Making," in *Oxford Handbook of the American Presidency*, edited by George C. Edwards III and William G. Howell (Oxford: Oxford University Press, 2009), 528–49; Stephen G. Walker, "The Psychology of Presidential Decision Making," in *Oxford Handbook of the American Presidency,* edited by George C. Edwards III and William G. Howell (Oxford: Oxford University Press, 2009), 550–574.

15. Plouffe, *Audacity*, 223.

16. Interview with the editorial board of the *Reno Gazette-Journal,* January 14, 2008, reported in "I'm No Bureaucrat," *Los Angeles Times,* January 15, 2008, http://latimesblogs.latimes.com/washington/2008/01/obama-makes-no-b.html.

17. "Remarks by Barack Obama in Nevada Democratic Caucus," *New York Times,* January 15, 2008, www.nytimes.com/2008/01/15/us/politics/15demdebate-transcript.html.

18. These include assistants to the president for economic, domestic, and national security policy plus the heads of the White House offices of Energy and Climate Change, Faith-Based Initiatives and Neighborhood Partnership, Health Reform, National AIDS Policy, and Social Innovation and Civic Participation.

19. Doris Kearns Goodwin, *Team of Rivals: The Political Genius of Abraham Lincoln* (New York: Simon and Schuster, 2005).

20. David Remnick, *The Bridge* (New York: Knopf, 2010), 475–76.

21. Barack Obama, *The Audacity of Hope* (New York: Crown, 2006), 120.

22. In an interview with the *Winston-Salem Journal,* Obama responded to the criticism of his remarks on people being bitter: "If I worded things in a way that made people offended, I deeply regret that." Marc Ambinder, "Obama Regrets If He Offended, . . ." www.blogrunner.com/snapshot/D/3/3/obama_regrets_if_he_offended.

23. The reference to Mrs. Reagan was mistaken. She had consulted with an astrologer regarding her husband's schedule, but it was Hillary Clinton who allegedly had séances with Eleanor Roosevelt.

24. Jay Leno, "Transcript of Obama Interview," *Tonight Show,* NBC, March 20, 2009.

25. David Brody, "Obama Gets Heated on Born Alive Infant Protection Act," *Christian Broadcasting Network,* August 16, 2008, www.cbn.com/CBN news/429328.aspx.

26. David Leonhardt, "After the Great Recession," *New York Times Magazine,* April 28, 2009, www.nytimes.com/2009/05/03/magazine/03Obama-t.html (emphasis added).

27. David Remnick, "Testing the Waters," *The New Yorker,* November 6, 2008, www .newyorker.com/archive/2006/10/30/061030on_onlineonly04.

28. Kroft, "Interview."

29. Jon Meacham, "Transcript of Obama Interview," *Newsweek,* January 27, 2009.

30. Gates, a well-known professor at Harvard, had a confrontation with police in Cambridge, Massachusetts. Gates was trying to open the door of his home after returning from a trip. The driver of the taxi that Gates had taken was helping him. The police had received a report that two men were trying to break into a house. Gates and one of the police officers, who apparently did not believe that Gates was the owner of the house, had a heated exchange, and Gates was arrested. Gates' notoriety and the fact that he was an African American and the arresting police officer was white headlined the incident and brought it to national attention. Asked about the arrest the following day at a scheduled news conference, the president said the Cambridge police acted "stupidly". His remarks, criticized by local law enforcement officials, generated a public debate on the race issue. The president later tried to make amends by inviting Professor Gates and the arresting officer for a beer at the White House.

31. For security reasons, however, only fifteen people were given Obama's Black-Berry e-mail address. Peter Baker, "The Education of a President," *New York Times Magazine,* October 17, 2010, 47.

4

CHARACTER-BASED TENSIONS

"You're never 100 percent certain that the course of action you're choosing is going to work. What you can have confidence in is that the probability of it working is higher than the other options available to you. But that still leaves some uncertainty, which I think can be stressful, and that's part of the reason why it's so important to be willing to constantly re-evaluate decisions based on new information."

— Obama in Kenneth T. Walsh, "Exclusive Interview: Obama 'Never 100 Percent Certain' "*

". . . we've got to make good decisions based on the facts. . . . And I am not going to be distracted by—what's happening day to day."

— Obama in Steve Kroft, "Interview of Barack Obama on CBS News' *60 Minutes*"*

"It's [the job] exhilarating. It's challenging. . . . the decision making part of it—actually comes—comes pretty naturally. . . . the hardest thing about the job is staying focused. Because there's so many demands and decisions that are pressed upon you."

— Obama in Kroft, "Interview of Barack Obama on CBS News' *60 Minutes*"*

---

*Kenneth T. Walsh, "Exclusive Interview: Obama 'Never 100 Percent Certain,'" *U.S. News & World Report*, October 27, 2010. www.politics.usnews.com/.../10/27/exclusive-interview-obama-never-100-percent-certain.html.

*Steve Kroft, "Interview of Barack Obama on CBS News' *60 Minutes*," March 22, 2009, www.huffingtonpost.com/2009/03/22/obama-60-minutes-intervie_n_177854.html.

*Ibid.

71

Character-based factors have contributed to Obama's difficulties as president and have detracted from his leadership image and political capital. He believes that one of his principal roles as president is to set the country's policy vision, yet he has deferred to others in detailing that vision. During the first presidential campaign, he promised significant and innovative change, yet as president he constantly seeks common ground and expresses his openness to all ideas and his willingness to compromise. He wishes to be bold as a leader, yet his decisions as president have been, for the most part, centrist and risk averse. He has presented himself as a multiracial person whose life experiences have enabled him to understand and appreciate the plight of a broad cross-section of Americans better than other politicians, yet he often appears distant, nonemotional, and sometimes defensive in relating to ordinary folks.

The fit between personality, role, and performance is never perfect. There will always be some challenges that have to be overcome and contradictions that need be addressed. Moreover, situations evolve. Unanticipated events occur. As new perspectives emerge, older beliefs are challenged. Character-based rhetoric and behavior that seemed appropriate at the time of the election may no longer be salient. Adaptation to changing circumstances is usually required but it is often difficult for a public official set in his or her ways, ways that have contributed to previous political and policy successes. Changing one's priorities, beliefs, management style, and instinctive responses, on the other hand, may seem uncharacteristic and inauthentic to people aware of a person's previous responses and actions and who expect them to be repeated.

Both basic beliefs and operational styles can present challenges when they conflict with character needs, personal or political goals, or are exercised in nonanalogous situations. In Obama's case, much of the tension between his character, beliefs, and style results from the clash between the leadership imagery his presidential campaign has tried to project and the conciliatory manner in which he operates, between the magnitude of the change he has promised and the common-ground solutions he seeks, between his tendency to downplay emotional and gut reactions and his desire to empathize with everyday folks and show them he cares.

Obama wants to lead, serve as a model for others, and be an effective problem solver. His goals are to reach out and use his skills to change public policy to make it more equitable and beneficial for a larger cross-section of Americans, liberal views that clash with the conservatism that has dominated American public opinion since the 1980s. He also wants to emphasize commonality over differences, civility over angry confrontation, and compromise over resistance to change. He gets frustrated with ideologues with whom he finds it difficult to reason. He is an idealist who operates pragmatically.

Idealism Versus Pragmatism

Obama's values and goals are humanistic. He believes that it is possible for minorities to improve their conditions within a democratic political system, as he was able to do, so long as that system operates in an equitable manner. As noted in Chapter 2, Obama is an equal opportunity advocate; his objective is to reduce the economic and social inequalities and the political advantages that go along with them.

He infuses his idealism with an optimism fueled by his life experience and the political merits of encouraging hope over pessimism when running for office. But he is a realist as well. A student of American history, Obama knows that the quest for equality in politics and society has been met with considerable resistance from those who may be fearful of systemic change and those who benefit from the current system. Nonetheless, his upbringing, education, and professional experience, particularly his own political successes, inspire him to seek change within the system and by lawful means. As a community organizer, adjunct professor of constitutional law specializing in civil rights, and politician, he has used his adaptive skills to move to increasingly powerful positions from which he is better able to accomplish his larger social and economic goals.

To play by the rules, he has had to be a pragmatist. To some extent, pragmatism constrains his idealism. It limits the scope of the goals he has articulated and encourages compromise to achieve them. Obama believes that this compromise is the price that people who live in democratic political societies must pay for their right to be heard, to try to influence public policy, and to participate in the selection of representatives who shape policy outcomes. Pragmatism also contributes to legitimacy of policy by the support it generates for accepting the final outcome.

Pragmatism for Obama is also his antidote to the ideological certainty to which he so strongly objects. It facilitates the give and take necessary in a heterogeneous society if people are to get along with one another and be more accepting of policy change. Pragmatism requires patience. Pragmatism tends to produce centrist policy, more incremental than innovative.

Evidence of Obama's pragmatism has been his unwillingness to prescribe the details of his policy priorities and his willingness to conduct negotiations behind closed doors and to engage in protracted negotiations until agreement can be reached, even though the way those negotiations are conducted cloud the transparency in government he advocates.

Direction Versus Delegation

Obama desires to lead, serve as a model for others, and be an effective problem solver. His presidential campaign appeal, to change policy and politics, grandiose by any standard, is combined with a "yes we can" optimism that created unrealistic leadership expectations. He promised to be a transformational leader, to provide vision. Yet in running his campaign, and thus far in governing, he has left many of the operations details and policy specifics to others. He is a director who delegates. He has been a candidate and president for whom policy priorities seem more important than the specific provisions of the policy itself.

Delegation was initially tough for Obama when he first ran for office. David Plouffe, Obama's campaign manager for his Senate and later presidential campaign, initially told him to "let go and trust" his staff, to which the candidate replied,

> I understand that intellectually, but this is my life and career. And I think I could probably do every job on the campaign better than the people I'll hire to do it. It's hard to give up control when that's all I've known in my political life. But I hear you and will try to do better.[1]

And he did. During his presidential campaign, he generally refrained from getting involved in management, budget, and some tactical issues unless requested to do so by senior aides. The campaign had an end-of-the-day call in which the candidate participated, but it was mostly about message.[2] That the campaign was well run and successful limited the need for Obama's involvement in operational details.

David Axelrod described his boss as comfortable in his new job from day one.[3] Obama's confidence stemmed in large part from his conception of the president's principal roles: providing policy direction, making critical decisions, explaining them to the press and public, and building support for his policy inside and outside of government. Obama enjoyed each of these roles, and believed he had the capabilities to excel in each of them.

Obama associates problem solving and public persuasion, two of his most valuable political skills, with the transformational leadership he wishes to demonstrate. Not only does he place great confidence in his own judgment, but as president he also has learned to bestow confidence on others, to Secretary of the Treasury Timothy Geithner for the rules and regulations imposed on the finance community, attorney Kenneth Feinberg on executive bonuses in private sector corporations that have received government loans and payment of claims from the British Petroleum compensation fund, auto czar Steven Rattner on the operation of GM after its government bailout, and Attorney General Eric Holder on a range of judicial issues from the closure of the Guantánamo prison to the courts trying enemy combatants to the issuance of signing statements by the president.

Delegation within the presidency is obviously necessary. It enables presidents to tackle a variety of issues within a relatively short time frame and saves them time and energy that would otherwise be required for routine decision making. It also enables presidents to take and remain on the high ground, creating distance between themselves and their top aides, distance that can be used to deflect criticism. Thus in the Obama administration it was the aides' fault, not the president's, when they downplayed the AIG bonuses, when the head of his White House military office approved a photo fly-over of New York City without telling city authorities or warning the general public,[4] and when disagreement developed over the effectiveness and honesty of the Karshi government in Afghanistan.

There are, of course, dangers in overdelegation. Presidents exercise less control over the content of the final product. Their aides may act in a way that the president does not like but may have to defend. Aides may also disagree with one another. Even before Obama became president, critics pointed to the danger of a cabinet of rivals when he announced Hillary Clinton as his choice for Secretary of State, former Treasury Secretary and Harvard University president Lawrence Summers for his top economic adviser, and Rahm Emanuel, a strong and assertive member of Congress and former Clinton White House aide, to be his chief of staff.

Competition among political and policy aides is inevitable. The problem is that such competition can lead to disunity that becomes public in the form of leaks and "kiss and tell" articles and books. Early in his first year Obama urged his cabinet to keep their policy debates inside the administration.[5] He railed against leaks, railings that themselves were quickly leaked to the press.

The most serious internal divisions concerned the war in Afghanistan and involved Gen. Stanley McChrystal. McChrystal's confidential report requesting 40,000 additional troops was leaked to Bob Woodward of the *Washington Post,* as were retaliatory White House leaks. According to Peter Baker of the *New York Times,* "the president erupted at the leaks with an anger advisers had rarely seen, but did little to shut down the public clash within his own government."[6]

For a president for whom consensus is so important, disunity within it has been very upsetting.

> I think the American people understand that my job here is to get it right, and I'm less concerned about perceptions, about process, than I am at making sure that once a decision is made everybody understands it, everybody is on the same page, and we're able to move forward with the support of the American people.[7]

Vision Versus Compromise

Obama promised to be a visionary leader, yet claims he is open to all good ideas whatever the source. He exudes confidence in his decision making, but he also craves consensus. To some extent, a penchant for compromise and desire for consensus raise questions about the confidence Obama has in the merits of his policy decisions. Why compromise if the decision is sound?

In a democratic form of government, there are lots of reasons to compromise. Broader support may be necessary to achieve a certain outcome, particularly in situations in which power is divided among and within the institutions of government. Although President-elect Obama and his economic advisers believed that the amount of spending needed to stimulate the economy in winter 2008 was well over $900 billion, the president agreed to reduce that amount to less than $800 billion to gain the votes of three Republican senators needed to pass the legislation.

Compromise can also provide political protection. When President Obama demanded that everyone on his national security team agree with the decisions he made on troop levels, strategic goals, and an annual reassessment of U.S. policy in Afghanistan, he wanted to ensure that his own military leaders would not undermine his policy by criticizing it later or making additional requests for people and equipment.

Compromise can send signals about future behavior as well. When President Obama negotiated a deal with congressional Republicans to continue the Bush tax cuts, set to expire at the end of 2010, in exchange for an extension of unemployment insurance and some business tax credits, he was indicating that he understood the political implications of the midterm elections and would have to modify some of his policy priorities in light of the new Republican gains in Congress. He also was indicating a willingness to cut other deals.

But compromise has its costs as well, costs that can be measured by the policy changes the president has had to accept. In the case of the tax negotiations conducted at the end of 2010, the president had to accept a tax on wealthy families that he had promised to repeal. He also had to endure criticism by liberal Democrats that he had made a bad deal, too early, one that made him look weak and unprincipled. In this case, liberal Democrats believed that Obama's overly conciliatory attitude damaged his credibility and the transformational leadership image that he wished to project.

He faced a similar problem at the beginning of his administration, also with fellow Democrats. Although the president tried to reach out to Republicans and gained some public credit for doing so,[8] he received little Republican support and thus found himself dependent on fellow Democrats to achieve his policy goals. They, too, forced him to accept compromises he did not wish to make but had little choice. The closer the vote on a presidential priority, the more leverage individual members of Congress, particularly fellow partisans, can exercise with the White House.

For a president who desires transformational policy change, a common-ground policy outcome, even when successful, tends to result in incremental rather than innovative policy. By definition, common ground eliminates the most controversial elements with which people disagree.

Obviously, some flexibility is required, particularly when dealing across institutional boundaries. Too much blurs a presidential imprint; not enough can result in failed policy objectives. Obama, thus far, has tended toward consensus building as a mechanism for policy formulation, although the polarized political environment has forced him to do so primarily within his own party.

Rationality Versus Empathy

In assessing his qualifications for the presidency, Obama pointed to his good judgment and even temperament. Lacking executive, military, or national security experience, he obviously could not stress these aspects normally associated with presidential leadership. "On the issue of judgment, I absolutely think that the decision about who the next president should be has everything to do with judgment and character."[9] Naturally Obama saw his own judgment as superior to his electoral opponent's and a model for his own staff to follow.

As noted in Chapter 3, Obama's judgment is a product of his keen intellect and his willingness to listen and learn. His analytic skills and legal training have contributed to the rigor and rationality of his thought processes. A deliberative decision maker, Obama is cool and calculating.

"We can't govern out of anger," Obama said to Steve Kroft in an interview on CBS's *60 Minutes*.[10] He repeated the same refrain to Kenneth T. Walsh in an October 2009 interview for *U.S. News & World Report*: "[Y]ou've got to make decisions based on information and not emotions. . . ."[11]

Obama prefers to associate with people whose temperaments are like his. "What I want around me are people who are calm, who don't get too high and don't get too low, because that's how I am."[12]

Occasionally, Obama becomes testy, but rarely angry.[13] There are reports that he has shown his upset when his strategic decisions were not carried out as he wished, when internal administration discussions were leaked to the press, and when he was blindsided by public reactions and events. But for the most part, his public posture has remained calm and controlled, with only a few displays of emotions.

One such occasion occurred during his rehearsal of the address he gave on Martin Luther King Day in the week before his inauguration. When he got to the line that noted that forty-five years had passed since Dr. King's "I Have a Dream Speech" was made to the thousands who attended the March on Washington, he paused and briefly lost his composure, saying, "this is really hitting me. I haven't thought about this really deeply." With his eyes filling with tears, Obama excused himself and left the room.[14] According to reporter and author Jonathan Alter, he also teared up during this campaign when he missed being with his family and on hearing of his grandmother's passing.[15] After viewing the returns of the remains of U.S. military killed in Afghanistan, he said nothing for the entire return flight to Washington.[16] Later, at a meeting with his advisers, Obama said, "If I didn't think [deploying more U.S. forces to Afghanistan] was worth doing, one trip to Dover would be enough to cause me to bring every soldier home."[17]

Whether his controlled temperament is a product of his life experience (he got all the anger out in his teen years and again by writing his life story), his political knowledge (he knew that angry African Americans do not tend to win public office in multiracial electoral districts, much less in the country as a whole), his legal training (the importance of using reasoning and logic in argumentation), or simply as a consequence of deeply repressed emotions or extraordinary political maturity is less clear and, probably, less important.

Emotional outbursts of one type or the other do not comport with his self-control and the confidence that such control conveys. Obama believes that emotions cloud judgment and impede deliberations; they undermine the expertise and advice that the best and brightest minds can bring to decision making in government. Too much public anger can potentially threaten democratic order.

Nonemotive decision making, however, can pose several problems. One involves underestimating the extent to which emotions affect the judgments of people, including public officials, and motivate behavior of people within and outside the public arena. Another has to do with the president's empathetic responses to situations in which public emotions have been strongly expressed. During his first two years in office, Obama's advisers told him on a few occasions to show anger to mirror public outrage when executives of failing companies, bailed out by the government, received enormous bonuses and when the British Petroleum oil spill in the Gulf of Mexico threatened the livelihood of so many people.

Showing anger has not been easy for the president. Addressing a group of small business owners in the White House following the announcement of the AIG bonuses, Obama coughed and attributed his momentary speaking difficulties to the anger he felt about the executive payoffs. The audience laughed; the president didn't sound angry.[18] Similarly, when the Obama administration's response to the oil spill was compared to the George W. Bush administration's reaction to Hurricane Katrina in 2005, the president's aides said that he would "kick ass," a term he repeated without much inflection in his voice in an interview conducted during this period. However, the use of the phrase coupled with the obvious magnitude of the problem pressured Obama to act. He forced BP to establish a $20 billion compensation fund for those who suffered financially from the spill.

Not only has the president's overt rationality made it difficult for him to connect to people who react more emotionally than he does, but it has also made it difficult for them to identify with him. Obama's public posture has contributed to perceptions of elitism, voiced by his political opponents.

During the presidential campaign, he responded to such accusations by recounting his life story—an absent father, a mother at times on food stamps who pursued her own career in Indonesia while her son lived with his grandparents in modest circumstances in Hawaii, and later his work in poor African American communities in Chicago as a community organizer. As president, he deflected the criticism by telling moving stories that people recounted to him in letters, e-mails, and town meetings.

Not surprisingly, Obama rarely mentions his educational background at a prestigious private preparatory school in Hawaii, a first-rate liberal arts college in California (Occidental), and later his transfer to Columbia University and his Harvard Law School training, much less the two books he wrote that have brought him millions of dollars in royalties.

But because of public perceived tendencies of elitism reinforced by analytical style that makes him seem distant, Obama is concerned with staying in touch. Even before he became president, he was concerned about the bubble surrounding the president that distances the person in the Oval Office from the real world. Obama wanted to keep his BlackBerry for this reason despite concerns by the Secret Service that corresponding on it would pinpoint his location and might be a threat to his personal security. As president, Obama has also made it a practice to read ten letters and e-mails a day selected by his correspondence staff for their representative character; he frequently retells the stories he and his staff hear about everyday Americans. He uses these stories to embellish his speeches and recounts them in interviews to demonstrate his understanding and appreciation of real world problems. Besides, telling human interest stories is good politics and helps personalize the presidency.

But Obama has not been as successful as Ronald Reagan and Bill Clinton were in reaching out and showing his compassion. Reagan's everyday manner of speaking, along with the stories he told, conveyed an understanding of the problems that many people were facing and feeling in the 1980s. Clinton's ease with people, his personal charm, desire to please, and empathy connected him with average Americans, a connection that worked to his political advantage. George W. Bush commiserated on a very personal level with military families who had lost loved ones in Iraq and Afghanistan.

Despite Obama's inspirational rhetoric during the 2008 presidential campaign, he has not been able to convey the warmth and emotion of his immediate predecessors. His pervasive coolness, intellectuality, and nonemotive decisions and statements have made it difficult for some people who react more emotionally to situations and events to identify with him and for him to demonstrate that he feels their pain.

Boldness Versus Caution

There is also tension between Obama's ambition and his temperament.[19] He wants to be bold, to make a difference, but tends to be careful and cautious when doing so. Although he emphasized policy and political change during his presidential campaign, his operating style and personal manner have been less dramatic. Reconciling his message of change and his desire to make a difference, specifically his equal opportunity goals, with his political pragmatism, electoral ambitions, and need for public approval has been difficult.

For Obama, most of his risk taking has been related to his personal ambitions. He refers to his decisions to seek the Democratic nomination for Congress in 2000 against incumbent Bobby Rush, the 2008 Democratic nomination for president against highly favored Hillary Rodham Clinton, and his major speech on race following Rev. Jeremiah Wright's incendiary comments as instinctive, gut decisions, two of which paid off.[20] The loss to Rush in the Democratic primary obviously did not.

Obama's first executive order to close the Guantánamo prison and his initial agreement to release information, including photographs, on prisoner interrogation that occurred during his predecessor's term, were not successfully implemented. His campaign diatribe against special interest lobbying, including his refusal to nominate lobbyists for positions in his administration and new ethical rules of behavior, did not inhibit lobbying activities or change the way Washington worked. Similarly, his opposition to congressional earmarks had fallen on deaf ears until Republicans raised the issue on their own after their victory in the 2010 midterm elections.

The lesson Obama took from these experiences was to be even more cautious in his pronouncements and the policy that flowed from them. As previously noted, he has been careful not to get tied down by the details of his legislative priorities and foreign policy decisions. He has avoided timetables for assessing his progress. When he included one in his decision to increase troop levels in Afghanistan, he accepted language "as conditions on the ground merit," which gave him a way out.

A rational decision maker, Obama assesses the costs and consequences of policy judgments on the basis of self-study, collective deliberation with

policy experts, and an ongoing survey of the political environment. He rejects rigid time constraints for making most decisions. The final product usually includes some wiggle room.

On the other hand, Obama tries to demonstrate his assertiveness by articulating broad goals, pointing to progress, using his executive powers forcefully, much as his predecessor did, and increasingly, resorting to popularist rhetoric to show his toughness and at the same time energize his Democratic base. But how tough can a conciliator be? How much assertiveness can a policy maker exercise if the policy specifics are all subject to negotiation? In a nation that seems to be deeply divided along partisan lines, what impact does assertiveness have? In the case of health care reform, Obama's persistence and ultimate success generated an angry outcry by his political opponents; in the case of his relieving General McChrystal of his Afghanistan command, it did not.

Summary

There are inherent contradictions in most people's character, beliefs, and operating styles. They stem from the application of past experience to contemporary conditions, from success and failure in achieving personal goals, and from politics itself. Presidents operate in a fluid political environment shaped by history and culture, an environment in which ongoing interpersonal relations, unanticipated events, and other situational factors require them to adjust their ways of thinking, speaking, and acting to achieve their policy goals and maintain their political capital.

For Obama, the greatest character-based tensions have resulted from his desire to direct change and his willingness to delegate to others; his lofty social vision and real world pragmatism; his transformational policy and political goals and his common-ground approach, conciliator style, and collective deliberations.

Obama's rational and nonemotive decision making has also produced a gulf between public emotions and presidential empathy. That gulf, at times, has impeded his ability to connect, persuade, and mobilize the public. The inspirational leadership he provided in the campaign has given way to the explanation and supplication of an increasingly defensive president trying to explain the merits of his policy decisions in the absence of discernible economic improvement.

Perceiving his role as a policy visionary, he has left many of the details to others. This operational strategy has enabled him to perform a multitude of tasks and stay focused on the big picture. But it has also reduced his influence on the final product and at times damaged his leadership image. Obama's conciliatory style has had much the same effect, blurring his personal imprint, lengthening the policy-making process, and subjecting much of it to critical press scrutiny. But it has also given him flexibility and allowed him to contend with a variety of issues, positions, and personalities within his own party as well as ambiguities in public opinion. His confidence and temperament have contributed to stability in troubled times but not to increased public confidence in his leadership.

Obama's character strengths, his intelligence, insightfulness, and energy have enabled him to tackle a multitude of serious economic problems, the worst since the Great Depression, redeem a large number of his campaign promises in whole or part,[21] continue the fight against domestic and international terrorism, and begin the process of revitalizing America's prestige within the world community. Although the results of these efforts, their impact on American society, and their consequences for future government actions require time to assess, the policy accomplishments have been substantial.

Although character tensions have tarnished the leadership image Obama projected in his 2008 presidential campaign and brought to the White House, they have also helped ground that image in the realities of contemporary presidential politics. For Obama, the principal challenge is to lead a much divided polity and to show empathy, particularly for those who do not share his views of government, interpretation of American history, and the need for citizens to exercise social responsibility for their brethren. He has much less trouble relating to those who suffer from economic and social hardship of one type or another. Reaching those people who are less active politically, a feat that his 2008 Democratic campaign did so well, has also posed a problem for the administration, one that the president believes can be improved by a more focused policy agenda, more effective framing of the issues, and the political mobilization that the next presidential election cycle is likely to produce.

Judging from the polls during his first two years in office, Obama's personal character has fared better than his issue positions and policy actions.[22] That he has been more popular than his policies suggests that questions of character have helped more than hurt his presidency. The divisive political environment; the absence of a broad public consensus on substantive policy issues; and the high levels of distrust in government, corporate America, labor unions, the mass media, political parties, and among people of different racial, ethnic, and religious groups are at the core of Obama's leadership dilemma. In the next chapter I turn to these political problems and their impact on the Obama presidency.

NOTES

1. David Plouffe, *The Audacity to Win* (Viking, 2009), 8.

   Thomas E. Cronin and Michael A. Genovese suggest that the American people have paradoxical views of presidential leadership in a democratic political system. According to these authors, the American people want a powerful president but are simultaneously fearful of the exercise of that power; they desire a president above the crowd and of the crowd at the same time, a president who is skillful, even Machiavellian, but also a person who is empathetic and kind, someone with well-thought-out views who is also capable of learning on the job. Cronin and Genovese, *The Paradoxes of the American Presidency* (Oxford: Oxford University Press, 2010). See also Thomas E. Cronin, *The Presidency: Teacher, Soldier, Shaman, Pol* (Boulder, CO.: Paradigm, 2009).

2. Ibid., 223.

3. According to David Axelrod, Obama's senior political adviser:

   > He [Obama] had a very, I think, pronounced adjustment period as a candidate. He wasn't comfortable as a candidate from the beginning, and he had to learn how to be an effective candidate. There was no such run-up to this job. The day he sat down in that chair in the Oval Office, it was as if he had been there forever.

   Kenneth T. Walsh, "David Axelrod: Auto-Bailout, Torture Memos Among Obama's Toughest Decisions," *U.S. News & World Report,* March 11, 2009, http://politics.usnews.com/news/articles/2009/03/11/david-axelrod-auto-bailout-torture-memos-among-obamas-toughest-decisions.html.

4. Seeing aircraft flying low over New York City, people were reminded of the two aircraft that flew into the World Trade Center on September 11, 2001. Many were frightened and called police and fire houses to warn or ask about the flights. New York officials knew nothing; they had not been briefed about the flights.

5. Jonathan Alter, *The Promise* (New York: Simon and Schuster, 2010), 155.

6. Peter Baker, "How Obama Came to Plan for 'Surge' in Afghanistan," *New York Times,* December 6, 2009, 24.

7. Joel Achenbach, "In His Slow Decision-Making, Obama Goes with Head, Not Gut," *Washington Post,* November 25, 2009, A5.

8. Jeffrey M. Jones, "In First 100 Days, Obama Seen Making a Bipartisan Effort," *Gallup Poll*, April 24, 2009, www.huffingtonpost.com/2009/03/22/obama-60-minutes-intervie_n_177854.html.

9. "Transcript: Interview with Barack Obama," *New York Times*, November 1, 2007, www.nytimes.com/2007/11/01/us/politics/020bama-transcript.

10. Steve Kroft, "Interview with Barack Obama on '60 Minutes,'" CBS News, September 24, 2008, www.cbsnews.com/stories/2008/09/24/60minutes/main4476095.shtml.

11. Kenneth T. Walsh, "Exclusive Interview: Obama 'Never 100 Percent Certain,'" *U.S. News & World Report*, October 27, 2009, www.usnews.com/.../articles/2009/10/27/exclusive-interview-obama-never-100-percent-certain.

12. Ryan Lizza, "Making It," *The New Yorker*, July 21, 2008, 50.

13. David MacFarquhar, "The Conciliator," *The New Yorker*, May 7, 2007.

14. David Remnick, *The Bridge* (New York: Knopf, 2010), 538.

15. Alter, *Promise*, 152; Plouffe, *Audacity*, 367.

16. Alter, *Promise*, 152; When Obama was in Afghanistan, he met a soldier who had lost three limbs. Later he commented, "I go into a place like this, I go to Walter Reed—it's just hard for me to think of anything to say." Peter Baker, "A Wartime Chief's Steep Learning Curve," *New York Times*, August 29, 2010, A10.

17. Baker, "Wartime Chief's Steep Learning Curve," A 10.

18. Alter, *Promise*, 312.

19. In a 1996 interview with *Le Monde*, a French newspaper, Obama contrasted his temperament with his wife's: ". . . my temperament . . . leans toward risk-taking and ambition, and Michelle's instinct for stability, family and strong values." *Le Monde*, 1996, www.huffingtonpost.com/2009/01/10/le-monde-publishes-never_n_156876.html. Although the reference was directed toward finding the balance between a public and a private life, both Obamas acknowledge him to be the extrovert and she to be the introvert. (Ibid.)

20. Joe Klein, "The Full Obama Interview," *Time*, October 23, 2008, http://swampland.blogs.time.com/2008/10/23/the_full_obama_interview.

21. For an examination of how well Obama has fulfilled his campaign promises, see the study being conducted by the *St. Petersburg Times* at www.politifact.com.

22. "Topics A-Z: Presidential Ratings-Personal Character," *Gallup Poll*, www.gallup.com/poll/1732/Presidential-Ratings-Personal-Characteristics.aspx; "Topics A-Z: Presidential Ratings-Issues Approval," *Gallup Poll*, www.gallup.com/poll/1726/Presidential-Ratings-Issues-Approval.aspx.

5

POLITICAL IMPEDIMENTS

"I want people to feel connected to their government again, and I want that government to respond to the voices of the people, and not just insiders and special interests."

— Obama in Jann S. Wenner, "A Conversation with Barack Obama"*

"What I want to do is lay out the situation for the American people. And this is going to be a general principle of governing. No spin, play it straight, describe to the American people the state that we're in. And then provide them and Congress a sense of direction."

— Obama in John King, "Interview with Barack Obama"*

". . . part of my job I think is to bridge that gap between the status quo and what we know we have to do for our future."

— Obama in David Leonhardt, "After the Great Recession"*

---

*Jann S. Wenner, "A Conversation with Barack Obama," *Rolling Stone*, July 10, 2008, www.janns wenner.com/Archives/Barack_Obama.aspx.

*John King, "Interview with Barack Obama," CNN, January 16, 2009, www.transcripts.cnn.com/ TRANSCRIPTS/0901/16/sitroom.03.html.

*David Leonhardt, "After the Great Recession," *New York Times*, April 28, 2009, www.nytimes .com/2009/05/03/magazine/03Obama-t.html.

Most presidential contenders promise more than they can deliver. They do so to get elected: They think it is necessary to win. Sometimes they get carried away by their own rhetoric, by their desire to please and their need for votes, and they overestimate their ability to make and implement public policy as president. Whatever the reason, candidates enhance public expectations of their leadership, which in turn makes that leadership more difficult in practice. They also subject themselves to more criticism as the press and opposition point to promises unfulfilled, failed, and forgotten.

When projecting a leadership image, few candidates remind voters of Congress's role in the formulation of public policy, although a candidate may suggest that his or her particular experience has provided the skills to deal with Congress more effectively than his or her opponent. Few contenders talk about the constitutional framework and its status quo orientation. They do not do so for the reverence shown the Constitution and for fear that it would detract from their own leadership images. Instead, they keep the focus on themselves and emphasize what they will do if elected.

The worse the public perceives external conditions, the more likely the candidates will propose major policy change, blaming the current environment on the incumbent president and the party that controls the government—as long as it is not their own party. In 2008, the American people expressed considerable dissatisfaction with the economy and with the George W. Bush administration's foreign policy, particularly the war in Iraq.[1] That dissatisfaction fueled Obama's message of policy and political change. It also contributed to his desire to project an image that was very different from his predecessor's, one that he believed was more sensitive to the needs and interests of a larger cross-section of Americans.

Obama promised to be a responsible, visionary leader and a strong president, one who would bring the country together, move it beyond strident partisan politics, and achieve major policy change, in contrast to President Bush, who was alleged to have exercised too much executive power in national security affairs, too little oversight of the private sector, and was too rigid and ideological in his thinking. Moreover, Obama also promised to lead in a manner that accorded with the dictates of a democratic political system in which public participation would be encouraged.

Trying to live up to this type of leadership has proven difficult for Obama, not only because of the tensions I have just described in Chapter 4 but also because of the political and governmental framework in which he is forced to operate. The constitutional framework separates institutions and shares powers among them; the political system is highly polarized with no party having a clear and consistent majority on public policy issues; and finally, the public remains skeptical of government and attempts to enlarge its responsibilities within the domestic sphere.

Adjusting to the realities of contemporary politics required the newly elected president to lower expectations, which his campaign, his "historic" election victory, and "honeymoon period" had raised to unrealistic heights. It also forced him to modify the style and substance of his public rhetoric.

This chapter examines Obama's adjustment and its impact on his leadership as president by describing the transition from campaigning to governing and the difficulties that transitions pose for a new administration and particularly for Obama's way of communicating and connecting to the American people. I then turn to the constitutional, political, and institutional hurdles that presidents have to overcome and that Obama faced in his early years in office. Here I place emphasis on the political environment in which the president found himself and which seemed to change him more than he was able to change it. In the last section of the chapter, I examine public attitudes toward government and the resistance Obama met when he tried to build support for his domestic policy initiatives. My focus in this section is less on personality and more on the factors that constrain it.

Transitioning from Campaigning to Governing

Governing is harder than campaigning. It is multi-dimensional in scope and continuous in practice. It involves more people who exercise more power, make more decisions on more issues, and do so over a longer period of time than do political campaigns.

The organization in governing is also more complex and less subject to the influence of a single person than is campaigning. Government has a history, culture, and structure of its own. It is functionally oriented and constituency directed. It also tends to be relatively stable.

Campaign organizations are more hierarchial and tend to be more fluid in operation. Win or lose, most dissolve when the campaign is over. They, too, are task directed, but that task has only one goal: winning the election. Government, in contrast, has many goals. Stated in the Preamble to the U.S. Constitution, the goals of government often create conflicts with one another. It is the job of those in power to resolve those conflicts through their public policy decisions made in accordance with established rules and procedures.

Elections have a beginning and an end; they require coalition building, but only for one vote. Government also involves coalition building, but for multiple coalitions that change with the issues. In elections, the coalition needs only to be sufficient to win, depending on the rules, a plurality or majority of the electorate, or in the case of the president, a majority of the Electoral College; in government, however, a plurality or simple majority may not be sufficient to achieve policy change. In the U.S. Senate, a sixty-vote majority is usually required to enact legislation on most substantive policy issues.

Governing strategies are more complex than campaign strategies. In electioneering, strategies are designed on the basis of the current political environment and with a single end in sight: victory. Elections can be thought of as zero-sum games. Governing involves multiple goals, shifting coalitions, and compromises among officials that represent different political constituencies for different lengths of time.

In campaigns, candidates debate a finite set of issues on which they have taken positions and frequently designed programs. The basic messages that contain their policy positions are repeated with considerable frequency in speeches, ads, and news coverage. In this sense, there is not a lot of learning that takes place among the candidates and their advisers, although phrases and policy statements are continually tested and adjusted to make sure that they achieve the desired effect. The candidates are out-front, selling themselves and their ideas to voters. They work long hours and interact with many people, but they are basically single tasked.

The issues change more frequently in government. Over the course of an administration, problems debated during the campaign become less salient and solutions, proposed months or years earlier, less relevant and often less viable. There is a lot of on-the-job learning. Presidents are multitasked and continually tested.

Government is presumably more open, more accountable, and more broadly representative of the body politic than are campaigns. Candidates represent themselves and their parties. Public officials represent diverse constituencies, but they also make national policy; presidents represent the entire country, not just their partisan or electoral base.

For all these reasons, it is much harder to be a president than a presidential candidate. The tasks and responsibilities are much greater, the structure of government more controlling, the issues more varied over a longer period of time, and the public larger and more fragmented.

Candidates create leadership images; presidents have to *exercise* leadership. Candidates make promises for the future; presidents have to deliver on those promises. Presidents make decisions and take actions that have present and future consequences. Moreover, they will likely have to deal with problems that they did not create and cannot control in an environment that may be hostile to their exercise of power or to the policy that they wish to pursue. It is a tough job.

Candidates are judged on election day; presidents are judged every day. Presidents have a bully pulpit, but they also have increased exposure by a watchdog news media, political commentators, and their partisan opponents. Campaigns are fast moving, but government provides a more stable and steady target for the scrutiny of the news media and political opponents.

The Obama Transition

Obama was confident that he had the ability to be a good president and make sound critical decisions. He soon found out, however, that the problems were more complex and of greater magnitude than he indicated on the campaign trail. His rude awakening came during the transition when he was warned by his economic advisers that the economic downturn was deeper and broader than any other economic decline the country had experienced since the Great Depression. This warning spurred him to action even before he took office. Meeting with Democratic congressional leaders in December 2008, Obama urged them to release the second part of the monies already appropriated by the Troubled Asset Relief Program (TARP), authorized to bail out and build up credit-lending institutions; at this time he also told congressional leaders about the need for a large stimulus package to prevent additional job losses and the need to pump money into the sagging economy.

Following the advice of his chief of staff, Rahm Emanuel, "You never want a serious crisis to go to waste,"[2] the president-elect decided to use the crisis as an action-forcing mechanism to get Congress to move more quickly and comprehensively than it normally would. Obama also used the economic crisis as an umbrella under which he proposed to make a down payment on his campaign priorities of health care reform, reusable energy, and education.

Once in office, Obama evoked his executive authority to order the Guantánamo prison at which suspected enemy combatants were held closed within a year, prohibit the use of torture in interrogations of suspected terrorists, and release memos and other material on the clandestine activities of CIA and Justice Department officials during the previous administration in its implementation of the war on terrorism. He also prodded Congress to enact the Recovery and Reinvestment Act that contained most of the economic proposals he and his advisers designed during the transition period. In short, he had begun his presidency in an assertive manner, proposing and directing the policy change that he had promised as a candidate and for which he believed he had a mandate from the voters.

Obama had also promised to change politics in Washington by reducing the influence of special interest lobbyists, improving transparency in government, and adopting a bipartisan approach to policy making. But his efforts were unsuccessful. He appointed several ex-lobbyists to positions in his administration, including the deputy secretary of Defense; his ethics adviser was "promoted" to an ambassadorship after six months in the White House and his office was abolished; he did not release all the pictures and memos he promised that described or illustrated interrogation methods conducted in the previous administration; and his appeal for bipartisan support fell on deaf ears. Congressional Republicans, unified in their opposition to the legislative policies that the administration was promoting, claimed that under the guise of bipartisanship the administration was really pursuing a partisan agenda in a partisan manner. Democrats, some of whom were unhappy with the compromises the president was considering, were also disappointed; liberals were upset at the pace of Senate deliberations while more moderate, Blue Dog Democrats were concerned about the amount of deficit spending and the significant increase in the size of the national debt. It was "politics as usual" in Washington.

A major component of the president's legislative strategy, bipartisanship, had become undone at the very time that another component of that strategy, restoring the institutional balance between Congress and the presidency by asking Democratic committee chairs to draft the legislation his administration wanted, was creating internal dissent, slowing down the legislative process, and subjecting it to greater and more critical press scrutiny. A third major component of that strategy, mobilizing public pressure on Congress by activating the Obama campaign organization, was also not working.

By spring 2009, the honeymoon was over. The Republicans, whose strategy was to oppose the president's domestic policy initiatives, began to gain the political advantage as President Obama continued to push his health care reforms and energy policy initiatives. Although the GOP lacked the votes to derail the president's proposals, its legislative leadership used parliamentary procedures to slow them down while Republican members of Congress and conservative political commentators went public with their criticism, focusing on health care.

Claiming the president's reform proposal was another big, intrusive, and expensive government program that would limit personal choice, increase costs, and damage health care services, Obama's opponents encouraged their supporters to attend town meetings and other forums to voice their opposition, much of which was very angry. The expression of strong emotion elicited news media coverage, which in turn fueled the anger and created a political movement, known as the Tea Party, the proponents of which viewed the growing federal debt, the intrusiveness of the national government, and economic and social policies of the Obama administration as serious threats to the country.[3] Strident partisan politics was reemerging in all its fury, and Obama was unable to reverse it or even tone it down.

The Obama Rhetoric

The bully pulpit wasn't working for Obama nearly as well as his campaign pulpit had. The reasons have to do with the differences between campaign and government rhetoric. As candidate for the presidency, Obama's job was to critique conditions, blame them on the policies of the previous administration and its political allies, and provide hope for the future. He had to sell himself, his policies, and to some extent, his party.

The sales job to people who identified themselves as Democrats, unhappy with the policies of the Bush administration, was not difficult, nor was an appeal to independents also discontent with Bush and his policies. Obama's rhetoric energized and broadened his base, helped by a very effective campaign organization and communications network.

Candidate Obama usually began his campaign speeches by repeating his life story, an unlikely one for a major party presidential nominee. The story referenced groups, events, and beliefs to which his audience could relate and at the same time provided them with a cause in which they believed and could participate—the historic development of a more tolerant, multiracial society in which equal opportunity for all was not just an ideal aspiration but an achievable goal. Obama's rhetoric embodied and emboldened the cause. Its inspirational tone and upbeat message discouraged careful scrutiny and analysis, although his opponents—Hillary Rodham Clinton in the primaries and John McCain in the general election—described it as more style than substance.

The atmosphere of the campaign permitted poetic oratory. Obama's cadences resembled those of religious leaders reaching and moving their

Source: © Jason Reed/Reuters/Corbis

U.S. Democratic presidential nominee Senator Barack Obama (D-Ill.) campaigns during an election rally in Henderson, Nevada.

congregations. Repetition reinforced the message of transformational policy and political change and the positive "yes-we-can" appeal.

As in most campaigns, positions and policies were directed toward specific constituency groups. Polling and focus groups were used to identify key phrases, design and target messages, and measure their effect, and if need be, readjust the message accordingly. Much of the campaign rhetoric and the heady atmosphere it created continued through the inauguration and into the president's first 100 days in office, the so-called honeymoon period. The press covered these events as if they were historic. Criticism of the president and his administration during this period was muted.[4] Although the harsh economic downturn was a reminder of the realities the new president faced, the news media emphasized the new beginning, new faces, and new policies.

Then political reality set in. The new president had to make decisions, take actions, build and maintain support, and provide leadership. His communication style changed accordingly. Information replaced inspiration;

Obama had to explain and persuade. He used facts, analysis, and logical argument to do so. Adopting a professorial style, Obama discussed the magnitude and depth of the problems the country was facing. Rhetoric describing the steep economic decline, the bail out of the too-big-to-fail corporations, the new signals given to the Muslim world, and the president's peace initiatives was much longer and more complex than the sound bites his predecessor had provided and the language Obama himself used in the campaign. The press had problems digesting his words as well as explaining them. The public, discouraged by the declining economic conditions, was not reassured. The sheen was wearing off.

The Obama White House gradually lost control of the public debate. The press began to evaluate components of the president's policy agenda more critically. Partisan opponents lashed out at the restriction imposed by government. Obama reacted defensively to the accusations. Although the White House made adjustments to its communications operation, both in terms of personnel and strategy, the news media kept its focus on the criticism the president was receiving. Obama began to understand the limits of the bully pulpit in the context of the contemporary news cycle.

A More Normal Presidency

Obama had been pushed off the pedestal on which his historic campaign and much-anticipated presidency had placed him. The nature of the job forced a change in the substance, style, and emotive content of the president's rhetoric.

In a politics-as-usual environment, Obama was forced to use more traditional political skills to build and maintain a governing coalition. He bargained and cajoled, as do most presidents, to transact the business of government and achieve his policy objectives. His policy vision had become mired in partisan politics and his transformational image reduced to that of down-to-earth president, negotiating deals behind closed doors to win votes. (See Box 5-1.) He had come face-to-face with the realities of presidential power—the office was not nearly as powerful as it seemed to be, or from his perspective, needed to be to achieve his policy priorities. Transformational leadership aspirations gave way to a transactional leadership style; the promise of unity was replaced by strident partisanship. Obama's policy goals had become mired in the political conflict between the parties and, to a lesser extent, within the Democratic Party. The president realized what he probably already knew, or should have known: that the American political system does not facilitate transformational leadership, except for short periods, usually in times of emergency. Without policy emergencies, presidents have difficulty being transformational leaders.

BOX 5-1 Transformational and
Transactional Leaders

Transformational leaders seek to change society in a major way. And they do so by virtue of their popular appeal, which acquires an intensity that differentiates it from the normal give and take of conventional politics.

Transformational leaders are inspirational, but they also need a public that is extremely dissatisfied with existing conditions or frightened about them, or both, a public that is willing to believe in and follow the leader. The power of transformational leaders resides in their ability to energize, mobilize, and command public support. They tap into the desires and needs of their followers. Often times, their leadership has a moral dimension to it that justifies their goals and the actions necessary to achieve them. Transformational leaders have a magnetism and stature that elevates them; their followers see them in larger than normal terms.

The rapid ascent of an African American to the presidency, a great accomplishment in and of itself, contributed to this imagery for Obama, as did his eloquent campaign rhetoric, which excited and energized his followers. In capturing and maintaining their support, the Obama campaign made them feel as if they were essential to the effort to achieve change in America. In addressing rallies, Obama substituted the generic "we" for "I" to enhance the cooperative spirit:

> This is a defining moment in our history. The dream that so many generations fought for feels as if it's slowly slipping away. We've never paid more for health care or child care or college. It's harder to save and retire. And most of all, we've lost faith that our leaders can or will do anything about it.
>
> But it is because of their failures that this moment of challenge is also a moment of opportunity. We have a chance to bring the country together in a new majority—to finally tackle problems that Washington has ignored for too long.*

In contrast, transactional leaders deal and bargain with others whose support they need to achieve their policy and political objectives. They trade benefits they have and others want for what they need: votes, endorsements, and active political support. Most leadership in a democracy is transactional, part of the give and take of contemporary politics.

---

*"Obama Plan for America: Blueprint for Change," www.barackobama.com/issues/index_campaign.php.

The Limits of Presidential Power

The problems Obama has encountered in redeeming his campaign promises and exercising presidential power are systemic, political, and institutional. The systemic constraints are constitutional, placed there by the Framers to prevent the accumulation of power in any one institution. The political constraints flow from the nature of the party system, and the institutional ones from the diverse representative character of government in the United States. In both political and institutional arenas, the personal needs and desires of elected officials play major roles.

The Constitutional Framework

The constitutional framework was not designed to facilitate executive leadership but to limit it most of the time, a proposition that a professor of constitutional law would obviously understand and appreciate. America's governing institutions were given powers and responsibilities to check and balance each other, powers used to protect their turfs from encroachment. They were "invited to struggle."[5]

Reinforcing this design was the federal structure of government, which includes spheres of shared and exclusive powers between the national government and the states. The governmental struggle thus occurs on multiple levels, often simultaneously, involving diverse individuals and groups seeking to promote their own beliefs and interests.

Federalism also worked to decentralize power once political parties were created. A state-based party system has evolved that has decreased the clout of national party leaders and increased that of state party leaders and the electorate that supports them. Both the separation of powers and the federal structure of government in the United States works to limit the reach of the president and the scope of executive authority.

A Polarized Political System

Since the 1980s, the partisan political divide has been widened by the increasing ideological differences between Republicans and Democrats, particularly among members of Congress. Obama, who seeks to represent mainstream, middle-class voters, has had to deal with a Congress that overrepresents the ideological extremes on both sides of the aisle.

The congressional parties are more unified today than they were during much of the twentieth century. That unity is good news for the president when the same party controls both houses of Congress and the White House, but bad news when government is divided. Obama was greatly advantaged during his first two years by large Democratic majorities in both the House and Senate. When the disputed Minnesota election was decided in the Democrats' favor and Sen. Arlen Specter defected from the Republican to the Democratic Party, Senate Democrats had the sixty votes necessary to prevent filibusters from derailing the president's legislative program. The Democrats lost that advantage after Sen. Ted Kennedy died in 2009 and a special election in Massachusetts resulted in the election of Republican Scott Brown. They lost control of the House of Representatives after the 2010 midterm elections and their Senate majority was also substantially reduced.

The partisan divide has affected perceptions of Obama, support for his policies, and approval of his performance as president. Divisions between Republicans and Democrats were muted slightly in the first three months following the 2008 election but quickly reemerged thereafter. With the economy in recession, the budget deficit and national debt growing, and the health care debate heating up, partisan evaluations of the Obama presidency became more pronounced.

Democrats continued to evaluate Obama's performance positively; independents became divided and increasingly critical of the president; and, not surprisingly, Republicans were the most negative. Republicans were much more opposed to the bailouts of GM and Chrysler than were Independents and Democrats.[6] On health care the split was even larger, with 81 percent of Democrats believing the legislation was a good thing and 86 percent of Republicans believing it was not. Independents were more disapproving (51 percent) than approving (41 percent) of the health care legislation Congress was considering.[7]

There were also major partisan divides over immigration and other social issues. When the president said in spring 2010 that he wanted Congress to enact immigration reform, two-thirds of Republicans wanted the legislation to focus on stopping illegal immigration, whereas a majority of Democrats wanted it to deal with illegal immigrants who were already in the country.[8] Wide differences persisted on such issues as gay rights, abortion, embryonic stem cell research, and the imposition of the death penalty.[9]

Only on the question of American forces in Afghanistan was their partisan agreement after the president made his decision to deploy 30,000 additional troops. Majorities in both parties supported the president's action, whereas a plurality of independents opposed it.[10]

On a personal level Obama fared better. He continued to be respected for his strong and decisive leadership, intelligence, and understanding of the problems Americans face. The public was divided on his management skills and whether he shared the peoples' values.[11]

Figure 5-1 Barack Obama Presidential Job Approval Rating, by Party

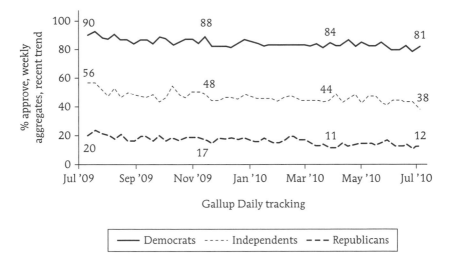

Gallup Daily tracking

Source: Jeffrey M. Jones, "Obama Job Approval Rating Down to 38% Among Independents," *Gallup Poll,* July 7, 2010, www.gallup.com/poll/141131/Obama-Job-Approval-Rating-Down-Among-Independents.aspx.

These issue differences, and to a lesser extent, personal assessments, were reflected in Obama's approval ratings during most of his first two years in office, which were the most polarized of any first-term president since the Gallup organization began using this measurement of performance. There was a gap of 65 percent between the average approval rating for Democrats (88 percent) and Republicans (23 percent) far exceeding the partisan divisions during the Clinton and Reagan administrations.[12] (See Figure 5-1.) Partisan polarization had deepened and solidified within the American polity.

Institutional Rivalry

The representational role that members of Congress are expected to perform provide them with a different orientation than the president has. An "all politics is local" perspective pits Congress's parochial outlook against the president's national view. So even when the president's party controls Congress, the goals and motivation that guide behavior of members of the House and Senate are different from those of the president, a point that a president whose only prior governmental experience was legislative must have realized even before taking office.

These differing perspectives are evident in positions that members of Congress take on legislation, the drafting of the bills themselves, and on the votes of members in committees and on the floor of their respective houses.

The president does have some leverage to influence Congress, however. Some of this influence stems from benefits that members of Congress desire and the president can provide, benefits that range from the expenditure of government funds in their districts and states to invitations to White House events to help in elections to the visibility of the bully pulpit. Presidents and their staffs have to be cognizant of these needs and desires because they will be expressed during the legislative process. Members of Congress require considerable care and feeding. Moreover, they do not like to be taken for granted, accusations that were directed against Obama's two immediate predecessors in some of their interactions with Congress.

The Obama administration was aware of how Congress operated. The president, vice president, and Secretaries of State and Interior were former senators, and the Secretaries of Transportation and Labor were former members of the House of Representatives. Emanuel, Obama's first chief of staff, had been the fourth-ranking Democrat in the House. Senior aides to powerful members of Congress had been appointed to top staff positions in the Executive Office of the President.

Obama presented his first-year legislative priorities to Congress in an address to a joint session on February 24, 2009, one week after he signed the Recovery and Reinvestment Act. The issue at the time of his speech was whether to move forward on other major and expensive priorities, such as health care reform and energy legislation. The deep recession and massive spending by the government gave some of the president's political advisers pause for thought;[13] they were fearful of overloading the legislative circuit. But Obama was determined to move forward. He regarded the status quo in health care, energy, and the environment as unacceptable. Moreover, he understood that his political majority in Congress would likely diminish after the first midterm election, just as it had for most presidents.[14] He believed the most opportune period to pursue these initiatives, which he had promised in his campaign and which were reaffirmed in the Democratic Party's platform, was during his first two years in office. In deference to Congress, however, Obama let the appropriate committee chairs write the legislation rather than doing so in the White House. He expected party leaders to coordinate that drafting process and move the legislation along as quickly as possible. The administration intended to exert its influence at the final stage of the process, during the likely House and Senate conference that reconciles the differences in the bills passed by the two branches. Such a strategy would enable the president to be flexible on specific parts of the legislation, minimize his involvement until the end of the process, and allow him and White House aides to make deals in the privacy of closed meetings.

The strategy, however, proved to be naïve and dysfunctional. It weakened the president, tarnished his image, dragged out negotiations, evidenced Democratic disunity, and encouraged and extended critical media coverage and commentary. It also made the president more vulnerable to the kinds of deals against which he campaigned and the kind of politics he said he would end, the politics of special interests.

Republicans remained unified in opposition, thereby making the president even more dependent on obtaining Democratic support. In criticizing the legislation, GOP leaders highlighted the sweetheart provisions that found their way into the stimulus and health care bills. Moderate Democrats, whose votes were needed for enactment, wanted the government's role and its expenditure of funds reduced. Liberals did not and were unhappy with the compromises that the administration already had made. For the president, the internal legislative politics turned out to be a political nightmare that lasted for more than a year. Deliberations over health care were conducted in full public view. During this period, confidence in Congress and the president and in both parties' national leadership declined.

Why would a newly elected president who wished to project a strong and decisive leadership image, a president who had confidence in his judgments, who saw his role as changing policy and politics, delegate so much decision-making authority to Congress? As an Illinois legislator and U.S. senator, Obama was certainly aware of the independent mindset of most elected representatives, their strong constituency orientation, and the difficulty of persuading them in public to follow his lead, particularly when they did not perceive it in their political interests to do so.

In remarks he made early in his presidency, Obama said,

As a former Senator, I believe that individual members of Congress understand their district best. And they should have the ability to respond to the needs of their communities. I don't quarrel with that. But leadership requires setting an example and setting priorities, and the magnitude of the economic crisis we face requires responsibility on all our parts.[15]

Why, then, did the president not take a more active, hands-on approach?

Obama's first mistake was overestimating the ability of his White House staff and cabinet officials who had served in Congress to influence the legislative process. His second was to overestimate his ability and that of his political organization to mobilize public support for his policy initiatives in the same way that they had turned out voters in the election. The president believed that he could pressure Congress from outside, but soon found that his opponents could do so as well. His third mistake was that he overrated the merits of his own judgment and the propensity with which Democratic members of Congress would follow his lead. Obama also overestimated the perception that the problems in health care, energy, and climate change would be viewed as crises by Congress and the American people, thereby enhancing the president's ability to gain their support.

Another contributing factor to the administration's willingness to let Congress draft the president's legislative priorities may have been the Clinton administration's experience with health care. The Obama White House attributed Clinton's failure in no small part to the comprehensiveness and complexity of the package the Clinton White House sent to Congress and its presentation as a *fait accompli*. The president wanted to avoid the congressional push back that stymied Clinton's bill. He also did not want to appear as if he took his party's support for granted, as George W. Bush had done with Republicans throughout most of his presidency.

For all of these reasons, the Obama administration gave up substantive control over the content of the legislation and operational leverage over the process. During the period of public debate and congressional deliberation, the president's leadership image was damaged, his approval ratings declined, and his political capital decreased. Few on Capitol Hill feared the president, thereby undermining the conventional wisdom that leaders must be loved and feared.

Public Attitudes toward Government

Obama's views on government were also out of sync with the public's views, and have been since his election as president. As noted in Chapter 2, Obama believes government has a responsibility to respond to emergencies, regulate the private sector, and promote the general welfare, particularly helping those who need it the most and are unable to exercise sufficient political pressure on their own.

The general public does not share Obama's faith in government. Trust in political institutions in the United States has been declining since the 1960s.

Table 5-1 Normative Perceptions of the Power of Government

Do you think the federal government today has too much power, has about the right amount of power, or has too little power?

	Too much %	About the right amount %	Too little %	No opinion %
2010 Sep 13–16	59	33	8	1
2009 Aug 31–Sep 2	51	39	8	2
2008 Sep 8–11	52	40	6	2
2007 Sep 14–16	56	36	6	2
2006 Sep 7–10	52	40	6	2
2005 Sep 12–15	50	43	6	1
2004 Sep 13–15	42	49	7	2
2003 Sep 8–10	43	49	7	1
2002 Sep 5–8	39	52	7	2

*Asked of a half sample

Source: "Topics A–Z: Government," *Gallup Poll*, 2002–2010, www.gallup.com/poll/27286/Government.aspx.

Table 5-2 Normative Conceptions of the Government's Regulatory Power

In general, do you think there is too much, too little, or about the right amount of government regulation of business and industry?

Gallup Poll	Too much %	Too little %	Right amount %	No opinion %
2010 Sep 13–16	39	27	21	3
2009 Aug 31–Sep 2	45	24	27	3
2008 Sep 8–11	38	27	31	3
2007 Sep 14–16	38	26	33	4
2006 Sep 7–10	36	28	30	6
2005 Sep 12–15	34	23	40	3
2004 Sep 13–15	37	24	34	5
2003 Sep 8–10	37	25	35	3
2002 Sep 5–8	35	31	31	3
2002 Jun 28–30	32	33	30	5
2002 Feb 8–10	28	30	39	3
2001 Sep 7–10	41	17	38	4

Source: "Topics A–Z. Government," *Gallup Poll*, 2001–2010, www.gallup.com/poll/27286/Government.aspx.

Confidence in governments is very low.[16] More people think the government has too much power rather than not enough of it. (See Table 5-1.)

They also think that there is too much government regulation of business. (See Table 5-2.)

These negative attitudes toward government have naturally affected evaluations of Obama's activist legislative agenda. With the exception of

Table 5-3 Public Concern About Obama's Use of Government

Do you think President Obama's proposals to address the major problems facing the country call for too much expansion of government power, the right amount, or not enough expansion of government power?

	Too much expansion %	Right amount %	Not enough expansion %	No opinion %
2009 Sep 11–13	51	37	10	3
2009 Jul 17–19	52	35	10	3

Source: "Topics A–Z: Government," Gallup Poll, www.gallup.com/poll/27286/Government.aspx.

his initial actions in dealing with the economic crisis, in which a divided public approved government intervention as a temporary measure,[17] the American public believes that he has empowered government too much.[18] (See Table 5-3.)

The persistence, even growth of conservatism, as the dominant ideological orientation, a cause and consequence of the antigovernment emotions, has contributed to the president's problem.[19] The absence of public support, combined with the president's inability to mobilize his base, has created a democratic leadership dilemma for Obama, one that we explore in the next chapter.

Summary

Most of the environmental problems Obama faced in his first two years preceded him in office: the rapidly deteriorating economy, growing inequities in wealth, two wars, and a decline in U.S. prestige abroad. The public mood was sour. At the time of his election, 75 percent of the citizenry believed that things were generally going in the wrong direction, 93 percent regarded economic conditions as fair or poor, 71 percent disapproved of the job President George W. Bush was doing, and 73 percent disapproved of the way Congress was handling its job.[20]

Obama had promised to change the policies that contributed to these undesirable conditions, mute the strident partisan politics that divided the American polity for three decades, make the government work again, and return hope and unity to the American people. These were big promises, but Obama consistently expressed optimism that they could and would be achieved in his presidency. His goal was transformational leadership. He created expectations that he was unable to realize in his first two years in office.

During the first three months, the so-called honeymoon period, economic conditions worsened. The deep recession combined with large Democratic majorities in both houses of Congress enabled the president to get a massive Recovery and Reinvestment Act passed as well as other bills that addressed aspects of the economy: protections for credit card borrowers, incentives to purchase homes and cars, help in preventing mortgage foreclosures as well as legislation to extend the Children's Health Insurance Program (CHIP), restructure weapons acquisitions, expand national forests, and give the Food and Drug Administration authority to regulate tobacco.

Then the realities of contemporary politics set in. As unemployment continued to rise, mortgage foreclosures accelerated, and the stock market lost about 40 percent of its value, the president's support began to decline. The news media became more critical. Republican opposition to more spending, more programs, and more government regulatory activity intensified, solidifying the party, and activating its base. Angry protests received considerable media coverage. People began to lose confidence that government in general, and Obama in particular, could solve these problems.

The GOP's electoral fortunes began to improve with victories in two off-year gubernatorial races, the special election of Scott Brown, a Republican, to the seat formerly held by Senator Kennedy, and finally by its large gains in the 2010 midterm elections. The Democrats had lost their partisan advantage.

The president's plight was further aggravated by his pursuit of health care reform and energy legislation, both of which became mired in the labyrinth of the legislative policy-making process. Obama's deference to Congress on these proposals weakened his political capital and leadership image.

Nor did the bully pulpit help the president's fortunes all that much. His inspirational rhetoric was replaced with detailed explanations; his multiple roles and tasks made it difficult for him to maintain a clear policy focus. The White House had trouble framing issues when Congress was still debating and negotiating the content of the legislation.

Republicans gained the media advantage by playing to the fears of their electoral base about government and the policies of the Obama administration.

The American people remained angry over the bailout of Wall Street (while its executives continued to receive large bonuses) along with unprofitable automobile manufacturers. The bailout also undercut Obama's populist rhetoric. If the investment community, the AIG insurance giant, the national banks, and the automobile manufacturers weren't special interests, then who were? In light of the dire economic conditions, the huge government expenditures, and public skepticism about government, Obama's activist agenda produced more criticism than praise. In two short years, the optimism of the electorate had turned into a pervasive pessimism with discontent directed at those in power.

Obama did not change Washington politics; he did not alter public views about government. Although people continued to respect his intelligence, his energy, and his generic goals, they became increasingly convinced that he would be unable to achieve them. The gap between Obama's words and actions on one hand and the results people expected on the other widened. In the domestic arena, the president no longer received the benefit of doubt. He faced a leadership dilemma that his personal attributes were no longer able to overcome.

NOTES

1. "Gallup Daily: US Economic Conditions," *Gallup Poll*, November 2008–July 2010, www.gallup.com/poll/110821/Gallup-Daily-US-Economic-Condi tions.aspx; "Topics A–Z: Satisfaction with the US," *Gallup Poll*, 1980–2010, www.gallup.com/poll/1669/General-Mood-Country.aspx.
2. Jonathan Alter, *The Promise* (New York: Simon and Schuster, 2010), 47.
3. Jeffrey M. Jones, "Debt, Gov't. Power Among Tea Party Supporters' Top Concerns," *Gallup Poll*, July 5, 2010, www.gallup.com/poll/141119/Debt-Gov-Power-Among-Tea-Party-Supporters-Top-Concerns.aspx.
4. "Obama's First 100 Days: How the President Fared in the Press vs. Clinton and Bush," Project for Excellence in Journalism, April 28, 2009, www.journalism .org/analysis_report/obamas_first_100_days.
5. Edward Corwin, *The President: Office and Powers* (New York: New York University Press, 1940), 208.
6. According to Gallup Poll data, almost two-thirds of Republicans were opposed, as were a majority of independents. Democrats favored it by a margin of 56 percent to 39 percent. Frank Newport, "Americans Still Not Buying In to Auto Bailout," *Gallup Poll*, December 9, 2008, www.gallup.com/poll/112993/ Americans-Still-Buying-Auto-Bailout.aspx.
7. Lydia Saad, "Verdict on Healthcare Reform Bill Still Divided," *Gallup Poll*, June 22, 2010, www.gallup.com/poll/140981/Verdict-Healthcare-Reform-Bill-Divided.aspx.

8. More than two-thirds of Republicans wanted the government's main focus to be on halting the flow of illegal immigrants, while 55 percent of Democrats wanted it to be on dealing with illegal immigrants already in the country.

9. "Topics A–Z: Abortion, Gay and Lesbian Rights, Death Penalty, and Stem Cell Research," *Gallup Poll*, www.gallup.com/poll/1576/Abortion.aspx; www.gallup.com/poll/1651/Gay-Lesbian-Rights.aspx; www.gallup.com/poll/1606/Death-Penalty.aspx; www.gallup.com/poll/21676/Stem-Cell-Research.aspx.

10. Fifty-eight percent of Democrats and 55 percent of Republicans favored the president's new policy in Afghanistan, whereas independents were divided almost evenly. "Americans React to Obama's Afghanistan Strategy," *Gallup Poll*, December 3, 2009, www.gallup.com/video/124583/Americans-React-Obama-Afghanistan-Strategy.aspx.

11. "Topics A–Z:" Presidential Ratings-Personal Characteristics," *Gallup Poll*, www.gallup.com/poll/1732/Presidential-Ratings-Personal-Characteristics.aspx.

12. Jeffrey M. Jones, "Obama's Approval Most Polarized for First-Year President," *Gallup Poll*, January 25, 2010, www.gallup.com/poll/125345/Obama-Approval-Polarized-First-Year-President.aspx.

13. Alter, *Promise*, 224–45.

14. The exceptions were Kennedy in 1962 and Bush in 2002. The president's party also picked up seats in 1998 following the Clinton impeachment.

15. Barack Obama, "Remarks by the President on Earmark Reform," The White House, March 11, 2009, www.whitehouse.gov/the-press-office/remarks-president-earmark-reform.

16. "Topics A–Z: Confidence in Institutions," *Gallup Poll*, www.gallup.com/poll/1597/Confidence-Institutions.aspx.

17. Frank Newport, "Americans OK with Short-Term Government Growth," *Gallup Poll*, April 15, 2009, www.gallup.com/poll/117523/Americans-Short-Term-Government-Growth.aspx.

18. "Distrust, Discontent, Anger and Partisan Rancor," Pew Research for the People and the Press, April 18, 2010, http://people-press.org/report/606/trust-in-government.

19. At the beginning of the Obama administration, 37 percent of the population identified themselves as conservative, 37 percent as moderate, and 22 percent as liberal. By the middle of the president's second year in office, 42 percent said they were conservative, 35 percent moderate, and only 20 percent liberal. Lydia Saad, "In 2010, Conservatives Still Outnumber Moderates, Liberals," *Gallup Poll*, June 25, 2010, www.gallup.com/poll/141032/2010-Conservatives-Outnumber-Moderates-Liberals.aspx.

20. "Exit Poll for Presidential Race," CBS News, www.election.cbsnews.com/election2008/exit.shtml?state=US&race=P&jurisdiction=0.

6

LEADERSHIP DILEMMAS IN A DEMOCRACY

"What the framework of our Constitution can do is organize the way by which we argue about our future. All of its elaborate machinery . . . [forces] us into a conversation, a "deliberative democracy" in which all citizens are required to engage in a process of testing their ideas against an external reality, persuading others of their point of view, and building shifting alliances of consent."

—Obama, *The Audacity of Hope**

"I am angry about policies that consistently favor the wealthy and powerful over average Americans, and insist that government has an important role in opening up opportunity to all."

—Obama, *The Audacity of Hope**

". . . we have been certified by independent groups as the most transparent White House in history. . . . We are the first White House since the founding of the republic to list every visitor that comes into the White House on line so that you can look it up. People know more about the inner workings of this White House, the meetings we have."

—Obama, "Interview of the President"*

---

*Barack Obama, *The Audacity of Hope* (New York: Crown, 2006), 92.

*Ibid., 10.

*Barack Obama, "Interview of the President" on YouTube, February 7, 2010. www.youtube.com/watch?v=0pqzNJzh7l.

In the last chapter, I noted the constraints on the presidency and explored the difficulty of governing in a large and heterogeneous society, with a constitution that divides power; a polarized political system; continuous institutional rivalry; a public suspicious of big government programs that are intrusive, expensive, and complicated; and policy outputs that are perceived as favoring special interests.

In theory, when Barack Obama began his presidency, he believed that the most appropriate way to combat these constraints was to mobilize a large, diverse, participatory base that would pressure public officials to design more equitable and efficient policy based on the common values, goals, and needs of the American people. His was an idealistic vision intended to make the practice of democracy in the United States more inclusive, the decision-making process more transparent, and public policy outcomes fairer to a broader cross-section of society.

In practice, Obama encountered difficulties that have precluded him from realizing this vision. The level of public participation has remained uneven. He and his aides have not been able to transfer the spirit, energy, and unity of his campaign into a viable governing coalition that is capable of mounting sufficient pressures on policy makers to offset the influence of entrenched, well-financed, and professionally-led interest groups. Nor has he been able to find much common ground with his political opponents or even with some of his electoral supporters.

Obama has not been able to reduce the partisanship that motivates so much of the behavior of public officials and affects evaluations of government by the general public. He has not been able to change public opinion in a significant way on salient issues. Instead of changing politics, politics appears to have changed him; Obama had little choice but to depend on his political allies if he wants to achieve his domestic policy goals.

Can Obama be the democratic leader he wrote about in his book, *The Audacity of Hope,* and articulated in his campaign, or must he be a Democratic leader who relies on his political clout and partisan advantage to shape public policy? Can he follow public opinion if it is divided, often ambiguous, with no apparent consensus? Can he convince the public by virtue of his own persuasive powers and his effective use of the bully pulpit that his priorities are important, his policies sound, and his actions justified?

In this chapter I will examine these questions, how President Obama has responded to the challenges they have created, and the kind of leadership he has been able to exercise from the White House.

Obama's Theory of Democratic Leadership

Obama is a democrat as well as a Democrat. As a democrat, he believes in participatory democracy. He writes about it, albeit briefly, in his book, *The Audacity of Hope,* talks about it in his speeches, and illustrates it by telling stories about ordinary people and their real world experiences.

In assessing American democracy, Obama identifies three principal concerns: the level of participation, the processes by which decisions are made, and the equity of those decisions. He frames his discussion of democracy within the history and structure of the U.S. constitutional system:

> . . . an Athenian model of democracy was out of the question, the direct democracy of the New England town meetings unmanageable. A republican form of government, in which people elected representatives, seem more promising . . .[1]

How to apply that form of government to a heterogeneous society in which minority rights needed to be protected was the challenge the framers of the U.S. Constitution faced. They eventually resolved this challenge by dividing powers within the national government and between it and the states and local governments.

For Obama the merits of the constitutional system lies within its framework, one in which democracy can flourish, elections can be held, and issues debated, ". . . a deliberative democracy in which citizens *are required* to engage in a process of testing their ideas against an external reality, persuading others of their point of view, and building shifting alliances of consent."[2] Obama believes that it is the job of those in government to make policy decisions in accordance with that public debate.

In practice, Obama notes that American democracy is a work in progress. It has taken vigorous dialogue, agitation, even violence over hundreds of years to broaden the conception of which citizens can participate in the electoral process and in the government itself. Obama's election as the country's first African American president testifies to that progress.

Obama believes that the democratization of the electoral process and the political system have been more successful than the equity of public policy outcomes. He sees the wealthy and powerful having a continuing advantage and is upset about that. Writing in *The Audacity of Hope,* he said, "I am angry about policies that consistently favor the wealthy and powerful over average Americans, and insist that government has an important role in opening up opportunity to all."[3] His view of a more ideal society is one that in which people believe that they can connect to a government that "responds to broad-based, public interests, not just to special interests.[4] According to David Plouffe, Obama's 2008 campaign manager, a primary reason Obama ran for president was to "reengage [Americans] in civic life."[5]

Participatory politics became the mantra of his 2008 campaign. He and his staff encouraged individual initiative and social networking. And these efforts were successful. Contributions soared, event attendance increased, volunteers supplemented the work of paid staff, and turnout expanded, particularly during the Democratic nomination process. The Obama campaign enlarged the participatory base of the Democratic Party during the election cycle. It had 13 million e-mail addresses, plus millions more cell phone numbers and zip codes on file, a file it preserved and gave to a newly instituted group, *Organizing for America,* with the objective of helping Obama govern. The plan was to mobilize his campaign supporters to pressure Congress to enact the president's policy initiatives.

Obama told Plouffe after the election, ". . . just make sure you find time to help figure out how to keep our supporters involved. I don't think we can succeed without them."[6] Plouffe recalls Obama saying,

> We need to make sure that they are pushing the grass-roots on Washington and helping to spread what we are trying to do in their local communities. And at the very least, we have to give them the opportunity to stay involved and in touch.... I want them along for the ride for the next eight years, helping us deliver on all we talked about in the campaign.[7]

The Bully Pulpit and Its Limits

Despite creating *Organizing for America,* Obama has not been able to energize his base as he had done during the 2008 campaign. And he and his aides have tried. Obama has used his bully pulpit more than any recent president. During his first year alone, he gave two major addresses before joint sessions of Congress; held 6 press conferences; gave 152 one-on-one interviews;[8] made 554 public remarks, statements, and comments to assembled individuals and groups inside and outside the White House—and this was all in addition to his weekly radio addresses. First Lady Michelle Obama, Vice President Joe Biden, and the vice president's wife, Dr. Jill Biden, have also been active within the public arena.

Obama continued to emphasize the public dimension of his office in year two. By the end of 2010, he had given 428 speeches and remarks, issued 245 statements, many of them hortatory, in addition to his weekly radio broadcasts, nomination announcements, disaster declarations, bill signings, and letters and messages to Congress. He held 5 news conferences and was interviewed by 5 foreign journalists.

Obviously, the president enjoys going public; he thinks he is good at it. He likes showing off his knowledge, confidence, and cool, collected manner. Moreover, he firmly believes that it is the president's job to teach and educate the American people. That belief is consistent with his desire to be a model for others who have not had the same opportunities he has had. Modeling requires visibility. Obama claims that public interaction grounds him in reality, a necessity for making pragmatic judgments. Keeping in touch not only allows Obama to escape from the White House bubble, which both elevates and encases the president, but it also enables him to compensate for a data-driven decision-making process in which policy experts debate complex and interrelated issues.

Obama is also confident—probably overconfident—of his persuasive abilities and teaching skills. During his presidential campaign, he railed against dumbing down explanations to the American people. Given Obama's rhetorical skills, his beliefs in a plebiscitary presidency, and his administration's major domestic policy initiatives, increased regulatory activities, and signals of international policy change, the amount of exposure he has gotten and the emphasis he has placed on the public dimensions of his office are not surprising. What is surprising has been the limited impact of these activities on public attitudes and opinions.

Lower Approval Ratings

Despite the extent to which Obama has gone public and his administration has tried to reinforce his policy appeals with a public relations campaign, support for the president's policies actually decreased during his first two years in office. His job approval ratings have declined since the end of the honeymoon period. The public has been unhappy with how he has handled the economy (with many Republicans also complaining that he has not spent enough time on it);[9] his health care policy; and the increasing size of the federal budget deficit. (See Table 6-1.) From the public's perspective the president has done better on foreign policy, although his approval ratings have been modest even within this policy sphere. (See Table 6-2.)

Table 6-1 Public Views on Obama's Domestic Policy

Do You Approve or Disapprove of the Way Barack Obama Is Handling the Economy?

	Approve %	Disapprove %	No opinion %
2010 Nov 19–21	35	63	2
2010 Aug 5–8	38	59	3
2010 Jul 27–Aug 1	39	59	2
2010 Mar 26–28	37	61	2
2010 Feb 1–3	36	61	3
2009 Nov 20–22	44	53	3
2009 Sep 11–13	46	51	2
2009 Jul 17–19	47	49	4
2009 Mar 27–29	56	39	5
2009 Feb 9–12	59	30	11

Healthcare policy	Approve %	Disapprove %	No opinion %
2010 Aug 5–8	40	57	3
2010 Mar 26–28	42	54	4
2010 Feb 1–3	36	60	4
2009 Nov 20–22	40	53	7
2009 Sep 11–13	43	52	5
2009 Aug 6–9	43	49	8
2009 Jul 17–19	44	50	6

The federal budget deficit	Approve %	Disapprove %	No opinion %
2010 Nov 19–21	32	64	4
2010 Aug 5–8	31	64	5
2010 Mar 26–28	31	64	5
2010 Feb 1–3	32	64	4
2009 Sep 11–13	38	58	4
2009 Jul 17–19	41	55	4
2009 May 29–31	46*	48	6
2009 Mar 27–29	49	44	6

*Asked of a half sample.

Source: "Presidential Ratings—Issue Approval," *Gallup Poll*, February 2009–November 2010, www
.gallup.com/poll/1726/Presidential-Ratings-Issues-Approval.aspx.

Table 6-2 Public Views on Obama's Foreign Policy

Foreign Affairs	Approve %	Disapprove %	No opinion %
2010 Nov 19–21	45	49	6
2010 Aug 5–8	44	48	8
2010 Mar 26–28	48	46	6
2010 Feb 1–3	51	44	5
2010 Jan 8–10	47	47	6
2009 Aug 6–9	53	40	8
2009 Jul 17–19	57	38	6
2009 Feb 9–12	54	22	24

Source: "Presidential Ratings—Issue Approval," *Gallup Poll,* February 2009–November 2010, www
.gallup.com/poll/1726/Presidential-Ratings-Issues-Approval.aspx.

During Obama's first year in office, his job approval ratings declined from a high of 69 percent to a low of 49 percent. They averaged 57.1 percent that first year but have been consistently lower in his second, averaging 47 percent in 2010.[10] What's the problem: unsatisfactory conditions, faulty communications, and/or critical news media coverage?

Unsatisfactory Conditions

External conditions naturally affect a president's approval ratings. In 2009 and 2010, the recession was the most silent issue. Although economists claimed that the economic downturn ended in the second half of 2009, and many banks and large institutions lent money by the government paid it back, unemployment remained high, real estate prices low, and mortgages continued to be foreclosed. When the government's stimuli program ended, the economic recovery was tentative at best. Although people still blamed George W. Bush more than Obama for the unsatisfactory economic conditions, the longer Obama has been in office, the greater the blame he has received.[11]

The 2010 oil spill in the Gulf of Mexico made matters worse for the president. Although British Petroleum, the company that owned the oil rig that exploded and subsequently dumped oil into the gulf for three months, received the bulk of public and media criticism, Obama still got his share.[12] His administration's response to the environmental disaster was initially viewed as too slow and poorly uncoordinated by Louisiana public officials, comments that received extensive press criticism.

With the war intensifying in Afghanistan and unemployment remaining stubbornly high, there just has not been a lot of good news for the president to report, which partially accounts for the decline in his job approval ratings.

Muddled Communications

Obama believes that his difficulties within the public arena stem from his inability to stay focused on a single policy issue sufficiently to hammer it home to the American people, a problem that his partisan opponents have not had. As president, he has had to explain issues of great complexity while as candidate he could simply point to problems and indicate that he had a solution for them. The president's problems have been compounded by his delegation of bill drafting to Congress. It is difficult to defend a bill until the final legislation has been enacted. In addition as president, Obama's matter-of-fact explanations have not carried the same emotional impact as has the angry criticism by his political opponents. Over time, the president has been forced to use populist rhetoric to defend his goals and the policies to achieve them. The rhetoric helped unify and energize his base but did not extend it.[13]

In February 2010, the White House revised its communications strategy to respond more quickly and effectively to charges that the president was out of touch with the American people. In addition to the popularist rhetoric, the White House staged more public events outside of Washington with the president front and center, interacting with "real people" rather than being surrounded by men and women in business dress—his advisers, politicians, and group representatives.[14]

News Media Coverage

During the honeymoon period, Obama received favorable coverage from the news media, far more favorable than either of his immediate predecessors, Bill Clinton and George W. Bush, during similar periods in their presidencies. But after three months, the halo wore off, and the coverage became more critical. A study by the Center for Media and Public Affairs found that 59 percent of Obama's coverage was favorable during his first three months compared to 46 percent from May through July and 39 percent from August through December.[15]

The news media's focus also shifted. At the beginning of the Obama presidency, the press highlighted the president's personal leadership qualities, which were positively evaluated.[16] As attention turned to Obama's job performance and the policies he was pursuing, coverage became more negative. Of the major issues covered, the Center for Media and Public Affairs reported,

> The president's economic stimulus plan garnered the best press—49% positive—and the financial bailouts of various industries the worst—33% positive. On other issues, coverage of the administration's general economic policy was 41% positive, coverage of health care reform was 39% positive, as was coverage of the war in Afghanistan, and the war on terror received 34% positive comments.[17]

Press coverage affects public opinion, but it also reflects it. The increasingly negative reporting on Obama's presidency, which was still, on balance, better than that of Ronald Reagan, Bill Clinton, and George W. Bush[18] contributed to critical public evaluations of Obama. Of the major news networks, newspapers, and magazines that the Center's report covered, the president received the most negative coverage on Fox, a television network with a conservative political orientation.[19]

Obama's Practice of Democratic Leadership

The president has been unable to follow his model of participatory democracy. As previously noted, that model consists of an active and informed populous debating issues and an administration that is responsive to that debate and any public consensus that may arise from it. The problem with this model has been the absence of a public consensus.

With moderates sitting on the sidelines and Obama's partisan opponents more energized than his electoral supporters, what was the president to do? What kind of leadership could he pursue in the political climate in which he found himself?

The president had little choice but to go partisan if he wanted to achieve major policy changes that he proposed in his campaign. Although he did not abandon his bipartisan appeal after the Democrats lost their sixty-seat Senate majority, Obama's base consisted almost exclusively of congressional Democrats whose political beliefs and electoral fortunes were most closely tied to his. The president's oratory became increasingly progressive and programmatic. The costs of pursuing a partisan strategy were considerable. Obama had to involve himself in retail politics on Capitol Hill, interacting with individual members of Congress.

Behind-the-scenes activities increased. White House and cabinet personnel lobbied their fellow partisans on Capitol Hill. Constituency-oriented "sweetheart" deals, approved by the White House, began infusing the content of legislation. Despite the president's tirade against the lobbyists and their special interest politics, the administration made its own deals with interest group representatives, obtaining support for its legislative initiatives in exchange for promises not to pursue certain policies or regulations. (See the health care reform discussion in Chapter 7.)

In short, Obama led, but it was primarily only Democrats that followed. Despite Obama's belief in bipartisanship and his promise to reach out to Republicans and independents, he led in a partisan direction, and only later, after the GOP's victory in the midterm elections, did he acknowledge that he did not reach out to Republicans enough.[20]

Campaign Promises and Policy Challenges

Obama has been remarkably successful in fulfilling his campaign promises. According to PolitiFact.com, a database maintained by the *St. Petersburg Times* that evaluates the extent to which the president redeemed his campaign promises, Obama kept 91 of 502 promises he made during the campaign, made progress on 285 others, was stalled on 87, and broke 14 in 2009.[21] By the end of his second year, his record improved to 113 promises kept, 41 compromised, 79 still stalled, and 219 in the works.[22]

The White House also achieved a significant portion of its legislative policy agenda. In 2009, legislation was enacted to stimulate the economy, limit interest charges of credit card companies, help Americans who were having difficulty paying their mortgages, aid small businesses, regulate tobacco, expand the Children's Health Insurance Program, increase aid to veterans, extend wilderness areas, reform the Defense department's procurement process, prevent workplace discrimination against women, provide tax benefits for making homes more energy efficient, and Cash for Clunkers, which provided a cash subsidy to purchase a more energy efficient vehicle. According to the *Congressional Quarterly,* the president received more support from his party than did Lyndon Johnson in his first year in office.[23]

In 2010 it was more of the same, with national health care reform, a veterans' health bill, the extension of unemployment benefits and small business loans, subsidies given to first-time home buyers, and regulatory reform of Wall Street topping his list of legislative enactments that the administration supported. A compromise with Republicans that extended the Bush tax cuts, extended unemployment insurance, and provided tax credits to small businesses, a repeal of the 'Don't Ask Don't Tell' policy on gays in the military, and ratification of the START treaty with Russia on nuclear arms reduction was achieved in the 111th Congress' lame duck session in December 2010.

The president had changed policy but not politics. He had moved public policy closer to the vision he articulated in his campaign. The conditions that he hoped would follow from that policy vision, however, would take time, and in the short term Americans were impatient and dissatisfied. Presidents Reagan and Clinton had been in similar positions in their second year in office. Their economies recovered in 1982 and 1995, respectively; their popularity increased as a consequence. Both won reelection easily. Naturally, Obama hoped the same pattern would emerge for him, but the recession he faced was deeper and broader than those at the beginning of the Reagan and Clinton administrations.

Changing Perceptions of Leadership Traits

In addition to how well presidents redeem their campaign promises and meet policy and situational challenges, they are also judged on the basis of their personal characteristics. Initially that judgment is largely shaped by the image they projected during their campaign. Over time, it is also affected by the success in which they satisfy leadership needs and desires of the population.

Perceptions of Obama's personal attributes improved during his campaign and were highly favorable at the time of his election. A poll conducted by the Pew Research Center of the People and Press a few days following the election indicated that people saw Obama as ". . . as inspiring (81%), down-to-earth (73%), patriotic (70%), honest (68%), and well-qualified (58%)."[24] Evaluation of his attributes improved during the transition period and the first 100 days of his administration.[25] Democrats were enamored with him, and independents assessed him quite positively. Only Republicans were negative.[26]

Partisan differences began to widen as the health care debate heated up in the spring and summer of 2009, and the president's job approval ratings began to decrease. Public angst over the economy, deficit spending, and health care reform began to take its toll on assessments of Obama's leadership skills. Overall, however, his first year evaluations remained much more positive than negative.[27]

Obama's second year evidenced more deterioration in the president's personal image. Views of him as a strong leader declined. People saw him as less caring, less trustworthy, less well organized, and less able to get things done. Nonetheless, his character dimensional were still evaluated more positively than negatively. (See Table 6-3, which provides a personal dimensional comparison of Obama with Clinton and Bush).

As reelection approaches, presidential perceptions tend to improve. Not only does the White House and the president's reelection campaign project and reinforce the positives, but when compared to a real-life opponent rather than the image their campaign created and early years reinforced, most presidents tend to look better.

Democratic Compromises

Obama had engaged in a bottom-up campaign, helped by the emerging technology of the Internet. That campaign, in turn, was predicated on his belief "that we needed to build a campaign that had this [civic engagement] at its core. As a former community organizer, Obama felt in his gut, that if properly motivated, a committed grassroots army could be a powerful force."[28]

Obama's plan for civic reengagement was to build a public consensus and use it to pressure Washington to change its ways and its policies. By broadening the base of participation, he hoped that ideological activists would no longer be able to exercise the kind of influence that contributed

Table 6-3 Recent Presidents' Personal Traits

Evaluation	Bill Clinton Jan. 1993	July 1994	Aug. 1997	George W. Bush Feb. 2001	Sep. 2003	Aug. 2006	Barack Obama Feb. 2009	Sep. 2009	Jan. 2010	Jun. 2010
A strong leader	—	—	—	—	68	43	77	65	62	53
Not a strong leader	—	—	—	—	29	52	13	29	32	42
Neither/Don't know	—	—	—	—	3	5	10	7	5	5
Warm and friendly	90	85	—	67	70	—	87	78	77	68
Cold and aloof	7	11	—	21	23	—	8	16	16	26
Neither/Don't know	3	4	—	12	7	—	5	6	7	6
Well-organized	—	42	—	66	—	—	81	69	70	63
Not well-organized	—	53	—	22	—	—	12	22	23	32
Neither/Don't know	—	5	—	12	—	—	6	8	7	5
A good communicator	84	—	—	—	—	—	92	83	83	77
Not a good communicator	11	—	—	—	—	—	6	13	14	20
Neither/Don't know	5	—	—	—	—	—	2	4	3	3
Cares about people like me	—	—	—	—	56	41	81	68	64	60
Doesn't care	—	—	—	—	38	53	14	25	30	35
Neither/Don't know	—	—	—	—	6	6	5	7	5	5
Trustworthy	63	46	47	60	62	41	76	64	61	58
Not trustworthy	29	49	47	28	32	52	15	30	31	37
Neither/Don't know	8	5	6	12	6	7	9	6	7	4
Able to get things done	—	40	64	60	68	42	70	58	57	55
Not able to get things done	—	56	29	18	26	51	15	31	35	39
Neither/Don't know	—	4	7	22	6	7	15	11	8	6
Well-informed	79	57	—	62	59	46	79	70	69	67
Not well-informed	14	38	—	27	36	46	15	23	26	30
Neither/Don't know	7	5	—	11	5	8	6	6	5	4

Source: "Obama's Ratings Little Affected by Recent Turmoil," Pew Research Center for the People and the Press, June 24, 2010, http://people-press.org/report/?pageid=1744.

to their control of nomination politics. He also believed that a consensus in the public interest would overwhelm and eventually dominate narrower special interests, resulting in policy that better served the common good and general welfare.

Obama's vision has not materialized. As president, he has been mired in ideological politics and plagued by special interests that are able to use their resources to gain access, make their case, and exercise pressure on elected and appointed officials. In the absence of a discernible consensus, he has also been forced to involve himself in insider Washington politics and use executive powers far more aggressively than he had anticipated before taking office.

He has also been forced to modify his goal of transparency in government. Claiming his administration to be the most open in history, Obama points to the availability of visitor logs for everyone who enters the White House and meets with administration officials; the televised White House summits he has held on the economy and health care; open congressional committee sessions; and the frequent press conferences, interviews, and public appearances in which he and senior White House aides have participated, as evidence. However, his close working relationship with Democratic congressional leaders, his administration's lobbying on Capitol Hill, and the internal operations of the White House have not been subject to much public scrutiny, let alone transparency.[29] And although the president has been especially critical of unauthorized leaks to the press, his administration has also followed the practice of previous administrations, giving reporters of certain news organizations, such as the *New York Times*, the *Washington Post*, and the *Associated Press* special access when it wants the story of a particular policy decision made public.

In addition, the president's top aides have been active in making deals with interest groups to get them to support administration policy. In one such deal, the pharmaceutical industry was promised that the administration would not allow Medicare to negotiate for lower drug prices and would oppose the importation of cheaper drugs from Canada in exchange for $80 95 billion in drug price discounts and a $150 million advertising campaign in support of Obama's health care reform plan.[30] Agreements with hospitals and health care providers were also negotiated.

Summary

Obama's views of participatory democracy, which is at the core of his beliefs about government and civic involvement, and his actions as president, differ in theory and practice. In theory, he believes in an active and empowered public, informed and involved, debating issues and hopefully thereby arriving at a consensus that government officials would shape into public policy. Consistent with this objective, he promised to raise the level of dialogue and reduce the amount of strident partisan rhetoric that has plagued contemporary American politics for the last several decades.

Obama built his campaign organization on the premise of citizen empowerment. Once elected, he wanted to convert it into a governing coalition that would actively support his policy initiatives that he believed would be beneficial to society as a whole, not just the special interests. To achieve this objective, he promised not to hire lobbyists, establish codes of conduct for his administration, and bring decision making into the open. Transparency and accountability were to be hallmarks of his presidency.

Obama has succeeded in changing policy, but he has not been able to do so according to the democratic model he espoused. He has not been able to maintain the participatory momentum that his campaign generated. He has not been able to follow issue-based public opinion because that opinion has been divided. He has tried to educate the public by persuading people of the merits of the legislative enactments, but has been unable to do so because of suspicions about government, concerns about deficits, persistently weak economic conditions, and few discernible indicators that policy changes were producing the desired results. As a consequence, public evaluations of his presidency have suffered, his governing coalition has been narrowed to Democratic lawmakers, and his electoral base has shrunk as well. Moreover, he has been forced to use traditional political skills and make traditional political deals to keep that base placated.

The transformation of Obama's democratic leadership goals into Democrat Obama's political leadership needs has not been easy for the president. In the short run this transformation has exacerbated political divisions rather than muted them; it has changed policy, but the long-term consequences of those changes are not clear.

The president has faith in his judgment. He believes that his policy will become effective and that the public will see its benefits. He hopes this will be accomplished well before the next presidential election. If Obama is right, and his policy improves conditions and perceptions that follow from them, his presidential evaluation and leadership image will also get better. It is much less likely, however, that his beliefs about civic engagement, extended and enlightened public policy debate, and a consensus on policy in the public interest will be realized.

NOTES

1. Barack Obama, *The Audacity of Hope* (New York: Crown, 2006), 87.
2. Ibid., 92 (emphasis added).
3. Ibid, 10.
4. Jann S. Wenner, "A Conversation with Barack Obama," *Rolling Stone*, July 10, 2008, www.jannswenner.com/Archives/Barack_Obama.aspx.
5. David Plouffe, *The Audacity to Win* (Viking, 2009), 20-21.
6. Ibid., 384.
7. Ibid.
8. Jonathan Alter, *The Promise* (New York: Simon and Schuster, 2010), 280.
9. Frank Newport, "Six in 10 Say Obama Has Spent Too Little Time on Economy," *Gallup Poll*, February 10, 2010, www.gallup.com/poll/125774/Six-Say-Obama-Spent-Little-Time-Economy.aspx.
10. "Topics A–Z: Presidential Approval Ratings," *Gallup Poll*, www.gallup.com/poll/124922/Presidential-Approval-Center.aspx.
11. Lydia Saad, "Bush Still Gets More Blame for Economy Than Obama," *Gallup Poll*, April 21, 2010, www.gallup.com/poll/127472/Bush-Gets-More-Blame-Economy-Obama.aspx.
12. Frank Newport, "Obama Receives 44% Approval on Oil Spill While BP Gets 16%," *Gallup Poll*, June 21, 2010, www.gallup.com/poll/140957/Obama-Receives-Approval-Oil-Spill-Gets.aspx.
13. Jeffrey M. Jones, "Obama Job Approval Rating Down to 38% Among Independents," *Gallup Poll*, July 7, 2010, www.gallup.com/poll/141131/Obama-Job-Approval-Rating-Down-Among-Independents.aspx.
14. Michael D. Shear "White House Revamps Communications Strategy," *Washington Post*, February 15, 2010, www.washingtonpost.com/wp-dyn/content/article/2010/02/14/AR2010021403550.html.
15. "White House Watch: Obama's First Year," *Media Monitor* 24 (Quarter 1, 2010), http://cmpa.com/pdf/media_monitor_q1_2010pdf.
16. The evaluation of Obama's first 100 days in office by the Project for Excellence in Journalism indicated that about twice as much of the coverage of Obama was concentrated on his personal and leadership qualities, 44 percent of the stories, than was the case for Bush or Clinton. "Obama's First 100 Days: How the President Fared in the Press vs. Clinton and Bush," Project for Excellence in Journalism, April 28, 2009, www.journalism.org/analysis_report/obamas_first_100_days.
17. "Obama's Media Image—Compared to What?" Center for Media and Public Affairs, Press Release, January 25, 2010, www.cmpa.com/media_room_press_1_25_10.html.

18. "White House Watch," *Media Monitor,* 24 (Quarter 1, 2010), http://cmpa .com/pdf/media_monitor_q1_2010pdf.

19. The report analyzed the evening news shows of the three broadcast networks, the front page of the *New York Times, Newsweek,* and *Time,* and Fox News Channel's *Special Report with Bret Baier,* "Obama's Media Image—Compared to What?" Center for Media and Public Affairs. www.cmpa.com/media_room_ press_1_25_10.html.

20. "Obama Tells Republicans He Should Have Worked More with Them," CNN, November 30, 2010, http://edition.cnn.com/2010/POLITICS/11/30/obama .congressional.leaders/index.html.

21. Bill Adair and Angie Drobnic Holan, "Rating Obama's Promises at the 1-year Mark," PolitiFact.com, January 14, 2010, www.politifact.com/truth-o-meter/ article/2010/jan/14/rating-obamas-promises-1-year-mark/.

22. "The Obameter: Tracking Obama's Campaign Promises," PolitiFact.com. www.politifact.com/truth-o-meter/promises.

23. Of the 151 votes that Congress took on which Obama had taken a position ahead of time, he won on almost 97 percent of them. Don Gonyea, "CQ: Obama's Winning Streak On Hill Unprecedented," November 28, 2010, www .npr.org/templates/story/story.php?storyId=122436116.

24. "High Marks for the Campaign, a High Bar for Obama," Pew Research Center for the People and the Press, November 10, 2008, http://people-press.org/ report/?pageid=1426.

25. "Obama at 100 Days: Strong Job Approval, Even Higher Personal Ratings," Pew Research Center on the People and the Press, April 23, 2009, http://people- press.org/report/509/obama-at-100-days.

26. Ibid.

27. "Obama Image Unscathed by Terrorism Controversy," Pew Research Center for the People and the Press, January 14, 2010, http://people-press.org/ report/?pageid=1643.

28. That growth had a very practical component as well. Running against a candi- date, Hillary Rodham Clinton, who was popular among Democratic activists and had the endorsements of many state and national Democratic officials, the Obama campaign had to grow the electorate that would vote in the Demo- cratic caucuses and primaries. And it did. Plouffe, *Audacity,* 20–21.

29. Alter writes that executive agencies have been slow in making more their records available. Alter, *Promise,* 427.

30. Ibid., 253.

7

THE INTERACTION OF PERSONALITY AND POLITICS: THREE CASE STUDIES

"Let's not play small ball. Let's make this [a new national electric grid] a national priority—it's gonna create lots of jobs."

— Obama in Jonathan Alter, *The Promise**

"Today, I'm signing this reform bill [health care] into law on behalf of my mother, who argued with insurance companies even as she battled cancer in her final days."

—Obama, The White House*

"Look, I think that you make sure that you have thought through all alternatives, and that you feel confident enough that this is the best decision, that it justifies potentially some of those kids [soldiers going to Afghanistan] not coming back. And the challenge is that you never have 100 percent certainty."

— Obama in Bob Woodward, *Obama's Wars**

---

*Jonathan Alter, *The Promise* (New York: Simon & Schuster, 2010), 90.

*Barack Obama, "Obama's Remarks at Health Care Bill Signing," *New York Times*, March 23, 2010, www.nytimes.com/2010/03/24/us/politics/24health-text.html?pagewanted=3&_r=1.

*Bob Woodward, *Obama's Wars* (New York: Simon & Schuster, 2010), 98.

"The conduct represented in the recently published article [comments by Gen. Stanley McChrystal in Rolling Stone magazine] does not meet the standard that should be set by a commanding general. It undermines the civilian control of the military that is at the core of our democratic system. And it erodes the trust that is necessary for our team to work together to achieve our objectives in Afghanistan."

—Obama, The White House*

Decision making is a product of multiple factors. A primary reason for conducting a study of character and politics is to understand how these factors, individually and collectively, affect judgment. What aspects of personality, politics, or the situation at hand seem to have the greatest impact on the decision—how quickly it is made, how strongly it is adhered to, and how others react to it? Was the president's response predictable?

To address these and related questions, in this chapter I explore three important decisions Barack Obama has made in his first two years in office:

- his decision to support a very large stimulus and reinvestment program to combat the deep economic decline he faced on taking office and at the same time, pursue policy priorities he advocated during his campaign;
- his decision to reform the nation's health care system despite the political opposition to it, divided public opinion, and Democratic electoral losses, particularly the special election in Massachusetts to replace Sen. Ted Kennedy;
- his decisions to deploy more troops to Afghanistan, redefine the war strategy and the timetable for implementing it, and subsequently change the military leadership prosecuting the war.

Each of these decisions set a course for the new administration, helped identify its priorities, established its operating style and philosophy of governing, and indicated the ways in which the president would interact with his supporters and political opponents.

The decisions also reveal a lot about Obama: the character of the man, his values and beliefs, and the way he relates to others. They also suggest the extent to which he directs and delegates, teaches and learns, and

---

*Barack Obama, "Statement by the President in the Rose Garden," June 23, 2010, www.whitehouse .gov/the-press-office/statement-president-rose-garden.

shapes and is shaped by people and events around him. Patterns, evident from these decisions, are likely to repeat themselves over the course of his presidency.

My objective is to discern how the person affects the office, and conversely, how the presidency and factors beyond it affect the person in that office. What follows illustrates, and to a large extent affirms, the analysis of Obama in the first six chapters of this book.

Stimulating the Economy

Every president wants to hit the ground running, but when to start and what can be done during the transition period is the critical question president-elects face early. For Obama part of the answer to that question was obvious on December 16, 2008, when he met with his economic advisers. Christine Romer, an economist on the faculty of the University of California at Berkeley, presented a report that she and Obama's economic team had researched and drafted. She began her presentation with an expletive-deleted phrase designed to shock the president about how dire the economic situation had become. The phrase caught the president-elect's attention as it was intended to do.[1]

Using government data on the gross domestic product for the third quarter of 2008, Romer described how quickly and deeply the economy was declining. The $150 billion stimulus package that Obama had proposed during the campaign would not come close to halting this downward cycle, much less reversing it. The president's economic advisers recommended a package of government spending totaling nearly $900 billion to prevent a "catastrophic failure," although they did not believe that even this amount would be sufficient to prevent, much less reverse, the projected economic decline.[2] The president's political advisers cautioned him that getting Congress to authorize a higher amount so soon after already spending $700 billion on bailout funds was unrealistic.[3]

The economic briefing the president-elect received lasted four hours. By the end of it, Obama had agreed to propose a large stimulus package, leaving his economic advisers to work out the numbers and the details. According to Ryan Lizza, a reporter for *The New Yorker* who interviewed the participants at the December meeting, "[Rahm] Emanuel made the final call: six hundred and seventy-five to seven hundred and seventy-five billion dollars, with the understanding that, as the bill made its way through Congress, it was more likely to grow than to shrink."[4]

Obama met with Democratic congressional leaders and their senior staff the next day to explain to them the urgency for so much spending. The president-elect was convinced that the extraordinary situation demanded an extraordinary response in an extraordinarily short time frame.[5] He left many of the specifics to Congress. He had to do so. As president-elect, Obama did not have the resources of the federal government at his disposal to detail the spending or draft the legislation. Besides, he believed that giving Congress discretion in writing the legislation would contribute to its enactment.[6]

The president-elect's decisiveness, which contrasted with the indecision and inaction of George W. Bush as the economic crisis unfolded, helped establish Obama's leadership credentials. It indicated that he would take charge early and that he would provide the vision and direction for the new administration.

Like so many of the decisions that followed, his early judgment was information-driven. It was set within a framework in which policy experts presented data, made recommendations, and reached a broad consensus on what should be done and how it ought to be done. Obama raised questions during the discussion, but eventually agreed with the judgment of his economic advisers that the crisis demanded a strong, unambiguous, and rapid response.

Political calculations were apparent in three aspects of the economic policy decision: using the crisis as an action-forcing mechanism to get Congress to legislate more quickly than it otherwise would; including provisions in the proposal that partially addressed three of the president's principal campaign priorities: energy, education, and health care; and giving congressional Democrats an opportunity to draft a bill that would benefit their electoral constituencies. That payoff, however, would be partially offset by the need for "shovel-ready" projects and by money given directly to the states to retain vital public officials, including police, fire, ambulatory, and other emergency personnel and teachers. Concern over increased budget deficits to which the legislation would contribute was overshadowed by the magnitude of the problem the bill was intended to address.[7]

Enacting the legislation also involved negotiations with Republicans. During the campaign Obama promised to listen to his political opponents and accept ideas that he believed would strengthen his proposal. In addition, he needed the support of at least three Republican senators to overcome a minority filibuster and get the sixty votes necessary to enact the bill. To gain that support, the administration and congressional leaders

Source: Saul Loeb/AFP/Getty Images

President Barack Obama speaks on the economy in Gaston Hall at Georgetown University on April 14, 2009.

agreed to reduce overall spending $878 billion to satisfy the demands of Republicans Susan Collins and Olympia Snow and to include $200 million in spending on medical research to placate then-Republican Arlen Specter of Pennsylvania. No other Republican in the House or Senate voted for the legislation. Although the president wanted Congress to pass the legislation so he could sign it into law on the day of his Inauguration, Congress did not enact the bill until mid-February 2009. With much fanfare, Obama placed his signature on the legislation on the President's Day holiday, February 17.

Despite the spending, the economic downturn continued, with unemployment reaching 10 percent and public confidence in the administration's ability to improve conditions declining. Bills to curb credit card interest hikes, aid mortgage holders, and regulate the financial sector had little impact on public opinion. Although the president explained the objectives and rationale for his policies, his explanation seemed to have little effect on public perceptions and altitudes.

Reforming Health Care

Health care had been an important issue for Obama even before he decided to run for president. As a state senator in Illinois, he sponsored legislation to expand a program that provided coverage for children without insurance. He later headed a commission that studied the expansion of health care coverage in the state. While in the U.S. Senate, he had voted to reauthorize the State Children's Health Insurance Program and supported programs that provided drug assistance to individuals diagnosed with AIDS, health care for survivors of Hurricane Katrina, and amendments to Medicaid and Medicare that broadened coverage and reduced individual payments.

Although he did not begin his presidential campaign with a detailed health care reform plan, he was forced to develop one early because of the salience of the issue for Democrats and the fact that his principal opponents for the nomination, Hillary Rodham Clinton and John Edwards, had promoted health care plans of their own that provided for coverage for all citizens. The initial Obama plan did not provide universal coverage for everyone except children, but it created exchanges in which people without coverage could seek it and those who could not pay the cost of the premiums would receive subsidies from the government.

Obama's health care plan in the campaign reflected his belief that the primary reason people lacked insurance was because they could not afford it, not because they did not desire it. Some Democratic opponents criticized the voluntary nature of Obama's plan. When he won the party nomination, he emphasized universal coverage as a priority. Health care figured prominently in his speeches, platform, and debates during the general election campaign.

Two years on the campaign trail taught Obama a lot about the issue and its impact. More important, it brought him into contact with people who shared their tragic experiences with illness, its high costs, and for those who had coverage, the problems they encountered getting their insurance companies to pay for the services they received. These stories mirrored his mother's experience while she was dying from cancer, when she received huge medical bills and struggled with her insurer to pay for them.

The health care woes Obama heard constantly throughout his campaign elevated the importance of the issue for him. Had it not been for the economic crisis, health care reform would have been his top domestic priority. As it was, it remained close to the top. And he included the computerization of health care records as part of his stimulus and reinvestment package.

Obama's choice of former Senate Majority Leader Tom Daschle as his principal health care adviser—to have an office in the White House and be spokesperson as secretary designate for the Department of Health and Human Services—indicates the importance Obama attached to the issue of health care reform and the confidence he had in Daschle, who had authored a book on health care after he left the Senate. When Daschle asked Obama about his seriousness in pursuing this issue in light of the economic downturn, the president replied that he hoped health care would become an important part of his presidential legacy. To reinforce his resolve, Obama asked officials from the Office of Management and Budget to set aside funds in his first budget for the health care initiative: He was that serious.[8]

Daschle's tax problems and the subsequent withdrawal of his nomination did not derail the issue for Obama, although it undoubtedly slowed attempts to start building a coalition of supporters within the industry, on Capitol Hill, and among the general public. *Organizing for America,* the postelection entity designed to replace Obama's campaign organization, had already sponsored living room discussions around the country on health care and how best to improve and support it.

Congressional Deliberation

As with the stimulus legislation, Obama made the decision to let Congress draft the health care bill rather than present the legislature with a comprehensive plan. The administration provided the goals and expected Congress to write the bill, using the considerable expertise of committees and their staffs to do so.

There were both advantages and disadvantages to delegating so much authority to Congress. The advantages were that the president could set the agenda without committing the time and energy necessary to work out the compromises necessary for enactment. Moreover, he could maintain flexibility on the contents of the legislation and his reputation would not be damaged if a particular item did not find its way into final passage.

With a full plate of other issues with which to deal, the president needed time. Delegating legislative drafting to Congress gave the president the breathing room that he needed and Congress pride of authorship. Obama hoped that authorship would give committee chairs more incentive to sell the final package to their colleagues on the Hill and to their constituents. In addition, it would put the president in a position to claim victory or defer blame to others, depending on how he liked the result.

The White House also believed that giving Congress leeway in designing the health care bill would help reestablish an institutional balance that members of both parties believed had been damaged by the unilateralism and assertive use of executive powers by the George W. Bush administration. They also wanted to avoid the Clinton health care fiasco when a finished product was presented to Congress as a *fait accompli,* a bill to be enacted rather than debated and amended. The Obama White House obviously did not want to repeat the process failures that occurred in 1991 and 1992.

But as noted in Chapter 4, there are dangers in too much delegation. The White House could not control the pace of deliberation; the president and his aides were not in a position to referee the jurisdictional battles among committees and the ego battles among chairs and ranking minority members. The delegation also opened up the process to greater press scrutiny and enabled the opposition to pick the legislation apart for the purpose of embarrassing the congressional Democratic majority and the president. Moreover, Obama was forced to be general in his public comments on health care until the contents of the legislation were clear, which was not until final passage.

When Republican criticism in May and June 2009 began to hit a responsive cord and generated angry public protests against the legislation Congress was considering, the White House began to lose control of the policy debate, and the president was placed on the defensive. He had difficulty responding to allegations, some outrageous, about the plan.[9] With so many other problems demanding his attention, Obama also found it hard to stay focused on health care, much less frame the legislative issue to his political advantage. Most problematic, he left himself in a position in which he almost had to accept the bill in whatever form it was drafted if he wanted health care reform.

Throughout, the administration maintained continuous communication with Congress, particularly with the chairs of the committees considering the legislation. The president was aware of the negotiations taking place between Sen. Max Baucus, head of the Senate Finance Committee, and Charles Grassley, its ranking minority member. Although the White House supported Baucus's attempt to reach some bipartisan agreement on the legislation, the president's advisers became increasingly concerned that Grassley and other Republicans on the committee were intent on stalling the bill. These concerns were heightened by critical statements about the legislation made by Grassley in the summer of 2009.[10]

In addition to monitoring the discussions in Congress, the president and his senior aides were engaged in deal making of their own, negotiating with the pharmaceutical industry and associations representing doctors, nurses, and hospitals. In exchange for their support of health care reform and contributions to the public campaign for its enactment, the administration promised not to use the Medicare system to bargain for lower prices or allow the importation of prescription drugs from Canada or other countries.[11]

Public Opinion

As the health care debate wore on, the American public became increasingly divided. When the president was elected, 64 percent of the public believed that it was the responsibility of the federal government to make sure all Americans have health care coverage, whereas 33 percent did not. When the Gallup Poll asked the same question in November 2009, the public was almost evenly split, with 50 percent deeming the provision of health care a federal responsibility and 47 percent saying it was not.[12]

The growing avalanche of criticism to the health care plan that Congress was considering had decreased public support for the legislation. Although a majority still favored reform, they did not see the issue in crisis proportions as Obama did. Nor did people see its relation to the present and future state of the economy, as the president did. In general, people who already had insurance or were seniors covered by Medicare did not believe that the reform would benefit them or reduce their health care costs. Worried about government spending and soaring deficits, such individuals also did not have much confidence in Congress, Democrats or Republicans; they had a little more in President Obama, but they were ambivalent about the role government should play in health care. Although a majority of Americans still favored enactment of health care legislation in the summer of 2009, partisans were deeply divided, with 79 percent of Democrats in favor compared with only 23 percent of Republicans.[13]

By September the divisions for and against a health care bill were almost even, with Republicans strongly opposed to the legislation and Democrats somewhat less strongly in favor of the legislation. People continued to be skeptical that costs could be cut and the quality of service improved. Many also feared that additional taxes would be necessary.[14]

Although polls indicated that President Obama was still trusted more than Congress, his trustworthiness was also waning. A majority did not approve of how he was handling the issue.[15] Public divisions on health care continued into November and December 2009. When asked in December of that year how they would urge their representatives to vote, a majority of people said they would ask their legislators to vote "no."[16] After the special election in Massachusetts to fill the seat of Senator Kennedy, a majority favored suspending work on the health care bill entirely.[17]

Opinion remained almost evenly divided through March when the House of Representatives voted on the Senate bill and modifications to it in the form of a reconciliation bill.[18] After the House voted in favor of the legislation and the president announced a great victory, supporters gained a 5 percent bounce, but one week later, the near-even division reemerged, with 3 percent more opposed than favoring the legislation. That division with more opposed than in favor continued through 2010. [19]

The administration was convinced, however, that once the health care bill went into effect, the public would see the benefits of the legislation. Just to make sure, they launched a five-year, $25 million, advertising campaign as the bill kicked into effect to tout its benefits.

The split in public opinion did not derail the president's health care initiative, but it did take the wind out of the democratic rationale for the legislation. Why would Obama persist in the absence of strong public support? His political advisers had raised flags of caution and urged him to cut back on the reform package, find parts on which there was some bipartisan agreement, and add to reform incrementally when the public was more supportive. [20] But the president was adamant. He told his cabinet in January 2010 during the football playoffs that he was on the two-yard line and did not want to settle for a field goal. [21] The issue had become personal for Obama. He saw the health care legislation as connected to his political capital and policy agenda, to the Democrats' ability to survive the midterm elections, to his presidential legacy, and most important, to a principal reason that he ran for president: to help those who needed help the most. The uninsured fit into this category.

Obama was also aware of the dangers of failure. Echoes of the Democrats' loss of Congress during the 1994 midterm election played in the heads of White House and congressional Democrats and contributed to their refrain, "Failure is not an option."

Finally, to get health care through Congress, the president would have to be fully engaged in the lobbying he detested and focus his public communications on this initiative to the exclusion of almost everything else. Planned events would have to be postponed. There would be additional burdens placed on already overtasked and overstressed White House aides. The president's leadership skills and reputation were on the line. On the evening of the Massachusetts' special Senate election, one that the White House knew that Democrats would lose, Obama met with Speaker of the House Nancy Pelosi and Senate Majority Leader Harry Reid to assess the situation and plan their outside and inside strategies.

Within the public arena, the White House waged a major public relations campaign in which the president participated heavily. His basic message—"the status quo is unacceptable"—was helped by a large California insurer that announced a 39 percent increase in insurance rates.

Source: Mandel Ngan/AFP/Getty Images

Obama meets with congressional leadership. Seated on the president's right is Nancy Pelosi and on his left is Harry Reid.

Obama had been scheduled to attend the Republican House Caucus near the end of January. The session, part of which was televised, went so well that the White House planned a follow-up bipartisan health care summit to be held at the Blair House across the street from the White House at the end of February. The administration clearly and finally was taking the offensive.

Even more important than the public campaign were the behind-the-scenes negotiations in which the president and Speaker were engaged. Their staffs had identified sixty-eight Democratic members of the House whose vote on the final package was uncertain. During a two-week period in March 2010, Obama and Pelosi met or spoke with each of these Democrats, who collectively controlled the outcome of the House vote.

Informed by their staffs of the reservations that these members had expressed both publicly and privately, the political dynamics within their individual districts, and any other relevant material, the president and Speaker framed their arguments. Obama offered help on legislative and political matters, including fund raising for the 2010 midterm elections. He also provided the stroking that so many in Congress desired. The Speaker did the same. It was a full-court press, one that required the White House to cancel two international trips and numerous domestic events.

In the end the president was successful in part because health care reform was his top domestic priority after the stimulus package was enacted. Helping people that were uninsured, people who on balance had little political leverage and needed the government to intervene on their behalf, was a major rationale he had given for running for public office, especially for the presidency. He wanted comprehensive health care reform to be a major part of his presidential legacy. That goal energized him and made him willing to go the extra mile. The personal stories he heard and not the polls he saw reinforced his resolve. An article in the *Washington Post*, written by Eli Saslow, told of a three-page, hand-written letter the president received on January 8, 2010, from Jennifer Cline, a young woman from Michigan, a campaign supporter, who had gotten pregnant, moved in with and married her boyfriend, lost her job and with it her health insurance, and then developed skin cancer. She wrote of the toll these events had on herself and her family. Obama read the entire letter and wrote back; he was moved.[22] He had received the letter a few days before he met with Reid and Pelosi on the eve of the Massachusetts vote.

There are other reasons, less emotive but still important to the president. Obama saw spiraling health care costs as a drag on the economy; he saw it as a middle-class issue with long-range partisan implications. Success would enhance his political capital, particularly among Democrats; it would work to reestablish his partisan presence on Capitol Hill and demonstrate his toughness, two perceptions that would contribute in the short run to his exercise of power. It would also help reinforce those dimensions of his personal imagery consistent with the presidential leadership traits he wished to project: strength, vision, empathy, persistence, and determination.

Finally, the large Democratic majorities in Congress provided the votes needed to enact the legislation. Pelosi's strong leadership combined with the president's intervention was sufficient to get a majority of House Democrats to accept the Senate bill and modifications specified in the accompanying reconciliation bill, a bill that only required a simple majority vote in the Senate.

Obama's success enacting health care legislation did not immediately change public perceptions about him, his administration, or the issue. Within six weeks, the BP Gulf oil spill would become another presidential leadership test. However, health care established a baseline from which he could be expected to push (not cave) and contributed to a record that voters would evaluate during the midterm and the next general election. Finally, Obama's legislative success kept alive the notion that a historic election had led to a historic presidency. He had transformed public policy, although the impact of that transformation would take years to be felt. In the interim, the fight over health care would continue as Republicans tried to repeal or weaken the newly enacted program in 2011 after they gained control of the House of Representatives.

Winning the War in Afghanistan

Barack Obama was mindful of George W. Bush's most fateful decision—going to war in Iraq. Critical of Bush's judgment at the outset, and determined not to make the same mistake in his presidency, Obama realized that he needed considerable information, knowledge, and insight before he could render a judgment as serious as the enlargement, modification, or termination of the war in Afghanistan. He also knew he had a short timetable. "I think I have two years with the public on this. . . . That's my window."[23]

Within the first two years, Obama was faced with four decisions on Afghanistan. The first were two separate requests from the Pentagon early in his presidency for additional troops to maintain order, oversee the conduct of upcoming elections in that country, and train additional Afghan security forces; the third was a report and recommendations from the commanding officer of U.S. forces in Afghanistan, Gen. Stanley McChrystal, for a large increase in troop strength; the fourth concerned derogatory comments that General McChrystal and his top aides made about senior administration officials who participated in the design and implementation of American strategy in Afghanistan and neighboring Pakistan, comments that were published in *Rolling Stone* magazine.[24]

The Initial Decisions to Send 17,000 More Troops and 4,000 More Trainers

About a month into his presidency and still not completely up to speed on the military, diplomatic, and internal political environment in which that war was being conducted, Obama made a decision, based on only two meetings with national security advisers monitoring activities in Afghanistan, to send an additional 17,000 troops. Five weeks later, following a NATO summit, he added 4,000 more to help in the training of Afghanistan's own security personnel.[25]

With the economic crisis consuming the bulk of the president's time, the administration was forced to defer to the Department of Defense's advice in its implementation of the war in Afghanistan. In May, Secretary of Defense Robert Gates, with the concurrence of the Chairman of the

Joint Chiefs of Staff Adm. Mike Mullen, relieved Gen. David McKiernan of his command of U.S. forces in Afghanistan and replaced him with General McChrystal, a combat veteran who had commanded Special Forces in both Iraq and Afghanistan. McChrystal was asked by the Pentagon to prepare a report on the war, a report that some in the White House (including the vice president) feared would force the president's hand in accordance with the military's timetable and strategic goals.

The lengthy secret report, sent to the Defense Secretary on August 30, 2009, was leaked three weeks later to Bob Woodward, the well-known author and assistant editor of the *Washington Post*. The leak put pressure on the president to decide quickly on the report's strategic recommendations. The White House, furious at the leak and the military's taking advantage of an inexperienced president, privately reprimanded top officers who they thought were responsible for it.

Redesigning Obama's Afghanistan Strategy

Despite pressure for the president to act on the recommendations in the report, Obama engaged in a comprehensive, careful, and at times contentious review of policy in Afghanistan. He convened strategic sessions of his principal national security team, that included Vice President Joseph Biden, Secretary of State Hillary Clinton, Secretary of Defense Robert Gates, National Security Adviser James Jones (as well as his deputies), Special Consultant on Afghanistan and Iraq Richard Holbrook, American Ambassador to Afghanistan Karl Eikenberry, White House Chief of Staff Rahm Emanuel, and the nation's top military commanders: Adm. Mike Mullen, chair of the Joint Chiefs of Staff; Gen. David Petraeus, head of Central Command; and Gen. Stanley McChrystal, commander of U.S. forces in Afghanistan. Eikenberry and McChrystal participated from Afghanistan via secure conference call.

The meetings, ten in all, began in late September and continued through late November. They were intense. Consuming more than twenty-five hours, they focused first on the situation on the ground, then on the U.S. mission and strategy, and finally on its planned implementation. The president was in no hurry to reach a final decision. *Newsweek*'s White House correspondent, Jonathan Alter, quoted Obama as saying, "My job is to slow things down," but when critics, such as Sen. John McCain, accused him of acting in too leisurely a way, Obama forcefully defended his decisional process.[26] "Nobody feels more urgency to make this decision—but to make it right—than I do."[27]

During these meetings, the president asked detailed questions of the participants, many of which required additional research by officials in the state and defense departments and analysts in the CIA. The only option taken off the table was withdrawal.[28] Peter Baker of the *New York Times* reported, "Mr. Obama peppered advisers with questions and showed an insatiable demand for information, taxing analysts who prepared three dozen intelligence reports for him and Pentagon staff members who churned out thousands of pages of documents."[29]

It was vintage Obama decision making: insightful questions, comprehensive data, and incisive analysis of those data, particularly with respect to how economic, political, and military situations interacted. The president led the meetings, asked detailed questions, reviewed and challenged assumptions of his advisers, directed the discussions, summarized the debate, and gradually built a group consensus on the policy.

There was considerable disagreement at the outset between hawks from the Pentagon and State Department, advocating the need for more force to handle the military situation and to provide a basis for assertive diplomacy in the region, and the president's more dovish political aides and the vice president, who reflected the concerns of liberal Democrats opposed to the war in Iraq, and saw Afghanistan through the same partisan prism.[30] Gallup polls in early November 2009 indicated that 57 percent of Democrats favored a reduction of troops while 65 percent of Republicans supported an increase. Independents were almost evenly divided.[31]

But this was not a decision in which partisan politics played a major role; it was one in which executive branch politics did, however, especially between the White House and the military. Obama was angry at the request for additional troops after he had already agreed to two requests, one to send 17,000 more soldiers to Afghanistan in February 2009 and another to deploy 4,000 trainers five weeks later. He was also upset about the leak of the McChrystal report and statements made to the news media by General David Petraeus and Admiral Mullen that he and his White House aides thought were intended to force the president's hand—hence the need for institutional push-back to reassert civil authority.[32] Obama was determined to signal to the military that he would not be as deferential to them as he believed that his predecessor, George W. Bush, had been. The problem was to figure out how to push back against the military and still accept their advice about the number of troops needed.

In the end, the president decided to send 30,000 of the 40,000 troops McChrystal requested and asked NATO to contribute the rest. Obama redefined the U.S. strategy from defeating the Taliban to degrading them sufficiently so that they would not threaten the security of the country, harbor al-Qaeda terrorists, and might eventually be persuaded to accept the Afghan constitution and reconciliation with the government. The president also set a faster deployment schedule for the troops going to Afghanistan and a timetable for withdrawing them beginning in July 2011, if conditions on the ground merited it. The new strategy and its implementation were to be reassessed in a year.

After the president arrived at his decision, he made certain that everyone of the principals that participated in the meetings was on board, stating "we're not going to do this unless everybody literally signs on to it and looks me in the eye and tells me that they're for it."[33] Obama felt he had to protect himself from internal criticism and public statements by members of his national security team, especially the military, statements that deviated from the plan. He also wanted to make sure that the strategy was executed in the way he wanted. To ensure that execution, the president dictated a five-page, single-spaced order that specified the strategy and its implementation.[34] He announced his decision publicly in a televised address from West Point on December 1, 2009.

This kind of agreement after discussion, debate, and judgment is an important requisite of Obama's decision-making style. He stresses team work and unity. Because he believes that the benefits of deliberative decision making cannot be achieved unless discussions are open, frank, and comprehensive—and unless all points of view are candidly presented and critically evaluated—he is intolerant of leaks that breach the sanctity of the decision-making system he uses.

The decision to send more troops to Afghanistan, the more narrowly defined war strategy, and the new timetables for deployment and withdrawal were consistent with Obama's pragmatic worldview, his hard-nosed, down-to-earth style, and most important, with his rational, argumentative, consensus-oriented mode of decision making. In a situation that involves American lives and treasure, situations that unleash emotions, Obama told Woodward that as president he had ". . . an obligation to work over, again and again and again, your goals, your mission, and your progress. Are we staying focused? Are we preventing mission creep?"[35]

Emotion was not evident in the decision making; it was slightly evident in the president's presentation of that decision to cadets at West Point. Obama had been moved when he visited the wounded at Walter Reed

Army Hospital in Washington, D.C., and the fallen at Arlington National Cemetery—hence his much quoted Veterans Day comment: "I don't want to be going to Walter Reed for another eight years."[36]

Obama's decision on the war in Afghanistan was consistent with his previous statements as private citizen, U.S. senator, presidential candidate, and president. He always believed that al-Qaeda and its Taliban sympathizers were the terrorist enemies that had to be confronted and defeated. One of his principal criticisms of the war in Iraq was that it took personnel, equipment, and money away from the war in Afghanistan.

Nor did the division of opinion among his Democratic base weigh heavily on Obama's judgment, although it did affect some of the initial advice he received from Emanuel, Biden, and others that advised his campaign and were part of his national security team. Nonetheless, the president did make a major effort to convince the Democrats and others who had reservations about getting more deeply involved in Afghanistan that his response was appropriate, sufficient, and limited; that the exit strategy written into the strategic judgment differentiated the operation in Afghanistan from Iraq and Vietnam. Polls taken after the president's decision indicated that a majority of Republicans and Democrats supported his judgment.[37] And they have continued to do so since then despite the increase in American casualties and the McChrystal incident.[38]

The Termination of Gen. Stanley McChrystal

Obama's fourth major decision proved to be the easiest and quickest. An article in *Rolling Stone* quoted General McChrystal and his top aides criticizing and belittling the vice president, the president's national security adviser, his representative to Afghanistan, the U.S. ambassador to that country, and indirectly the president himself. They also mocked the contributions of the French, NATO allies, to the military effort in Afghanistan.

When knowledge of the article became public, Secretary Gates ordered McChrystal back to Washington. En route, the general apologized for his remarks privately by telephone to Vice President Joe Biden. After meeting with Secretary Gates, McChrystal made a more public apology. He was scheduled to meet with the president the following morning preceding an already-scheduled national security session.

Within the White House, senior aides were debating what the president should do. There were two options: relieve the general of his command or reprimand him but allow him to keep his command so as not to adversely affect the war.

President Obama meets with Gen. Stanley McChrystal.

Meeting with McChrystal the next morning, the president listened to McChrystal's apology and then accepted his resignation. He then met with his national security team (without McChrystal). During that meeting, it was decided that General Petraeus, who had carried out the successful surge in Iraq in 2007, should assume command of coalition forces in Afghanistan. Petraeus, a participant of Obama's Afghanistan's strategy sessions, understood and supported Obama's strategic decision. His job was now to execute it.

Public opinion and partisan politics played relatively minor, if any, role in the McChrystal decision. Conservative commentators, members of Congress who had military experience, and foreign policy experts saw the general's comments as inappropriate at best and a violation of the chain of command at worst. They saw it as Obama's call, and few criticized him for it.

Obama needed to reassert his authority, and move forward with a unified team. "I welcome debate, but I won't tolerate division," the president said later in the Rose Garden.[39] But he also pointed out in those remarks that McChrystal's conduct "does not meet the standard that should be set by a commanding general. It undermines the civilian control of the military that is at the core of our democratic system."[40]

Summary

Personality and politics affect decision making, but they do so in different ways and at different times. In the first of Obama's major decisions—to move quickly with a major stimulus package—the president-elect and later, president, was responding to his economic advisers, who saw the American economy in freefall. He was also acting in a manner that was consistent with his belief that government must respond to national emergencies. As a president-elect without much national governing experience, he also had to demonstrate attributes that leadership requires and people expect: vision, resolve, decisiveness, and confidence.

Obama's decision on handling the economy with a large stimulus and reinvestment program enabled him to hit the ground running. It connected the campaign to governance in a way that showed a capable Obama ready to be president, with the intelligence and know-how needed for the job. The delegation of the details to Congress was a consequence of the calendar in which the new Congress begins before the new president, the expertise that established congressional committees have but which new nominees and appointees have yet to develop, and a judgment that Obama's congressional-experienced staff could work effectively with a Democratically-controlled legislature, a judgment that the administration has revisited during and after its first year in office.

The decisions on Afghanistan were also driven by the decision-making process the president had established. The schedule for those decisions, however, was initiated by military reports, recommendations, and in the McChrystal case, recriminations that forced an administration response. In the case of Afghanistan, White House–Pentagon friction and rivalry was apparent at the outset. Nonetheless, there was collective deliberation with the president guiding the discussion, achieving points of agreement, and arriving at a judgment to which the participants (including the military commanders) gave their assent and promised their support. In the process, Obama obtained a more nuanced policy, assertively redefined his relationship with the military, and produced a unified response that was accepted by a majority of the American people.

When that unification threatened to become undone by the publication of critical comments by General McChrystal and his staff, the president acted quickly and forcefully to silence and remove the dissident elements. His actions did not create deep cleavages within the polity or the political parties. Civilian control of the military remained a hallowed constitutional principle.

In both the economic and military decisions, reason trumped emotion. In fact, Obama had difficulties showing emotion associated with economic suffering; he listed statistics that revealed the magnitude of the problem and indicated what might have happened if he hadn't acted quickly and boldly. He did rail against the executive bonuses given by the bailed out American Insurance Group (AIG), but *said* he was angrier than he sounded. He also has had trouble evoking emotions associated with personal loss, although he claimed the war decisions were the hardest of his presidency.

Health care is another story. This issue became personal and political for the president. The anguish emanating from the health care problems of ordinary people pierced Obama's stoic temperament; stories he heard during and after the campaign moved him to action. Obama wanted health insurance as his legacy; he saw it intrinsically tied to his political capital, and his ability to address other legislative priorities. The personal dimension of the issue prompted him to go the extra mile and do what he dislikes, engage in retail politics behind closed doors. The cost was a concentrated two-month effort focused almost entirely on health care, requiring multiple promises and chits from the White House and some strong-arming by the president and Speaker in exchange for a favorable vote on the legislation.

As with the Recovery and Reinvestment Act and related legislative actions, Obama won the health care battle but did not initially gain public support for his actions. But he believes he will. And he strongly believes he has made good a policy judgment that will benefit American society over time.

NOTES

1. Obama is reputed to have said, "I just can't believe she just said 'shit.'" Jonathan Alter, *The Promise* (New York: Simon and Schuster, 2010), 88.
2. Ryan Lizza, "Inside the Crisis: Larry Summers and the White House Economic Team," *The New Yorker*, October 12, 2009, www.newyorker.com/reporting/2009/10/12/091012fa_fact_lizza.
3. During fall 2008, as the economy slid into recession and the credit crisis loomed large, Congress enacted the Troubled Asset Relief Program (TARP) and authorized $700 billion in spending to save large Wall Street investment and

insurance firms from bankruptcy. Proposed by President George W. Bush's Secretary of the Treasury, Henry Paulsen, the plan received the endorsement of both major party candidates in the 2008 presidential election.

4. Lizza, "Inside the Crisis."

5. Obama recalled, "[W]e had to work very rapidly to try to create a combination of measures that would stop the free-fall and cauterize the job loss." Jann S. Wenner, "Obama in Command: The Rolling Stone Interview," *Rolling Stone,* October 15, 2010, www.rollingstone.com/politics/news/17390/209395.

6. Alter, *The Promise,* 78.

7. The president did indicate in an address to Congress on February 24, 2009, however, that he was mindful of the deficit and the growth of the national debt.

8. Jonathan Cohn, "How They Did It: The Inside Account of Health Care Reform's Triumph," *New Republic,* June 10, 2010, 17.

9. Former Alaska governor, Sarah Palin, talked about death panels in which government bureaucrats would decide when to pull the plug on granny and when to determinate assistance for the very ill. Other critics talked about not being able to chose doctors, waiting hours for medical service, paying more money but receiving lower quality treatment. Some saw it as another entitlement program with big bureaucracies, high government expenditures, and the usual amount of fraud, waste, and abuse.

10. Liz Halloran, "Is Grassley Abandoning Bipartisan Health Bill?" *NPR,* August 20, 2009, www.npr.org/templates/story/story.php?storyId=112044867.

11. Alter, *The Promise,* 253–54.

12. "Topics A–Z: Healthcare System," *Gallup Poll,* www.gallup.com/poll/4708/Healthcare-System.aspx.

13. Frank Newport, "Americans on Healthcare Reform: Top 10 Takeaways: Key Findings from Gallup Surveys," *Gallup Poll,* July 31, 2009, www.gallup.com/poll/121997/Americans-Healthcare-Reform-Top-Takeaways.aspx.

14. Jeffrey M. Jones, "Majority in U.S. Favors Healthcare Reform This Year," *Gallup Poll,* July 14, 2009, www.gallup.com/poll/121664/Majority-Favors-Healthcare-Reform-This-Year.aspx.

15. Jeffrey M. Jones, "Many Americans Doubt Costs, Benefits of Healthcare Reform," *Gallup Poll,* September 16, 2009, www.gallup.com/poll/122969/Many-Americans-Doubt-Costs-Benefits-Healthcare-Reform.aspx. Frank Newport, Jeffrey M. Jones, and Lydia Saad, "Americans on Healthcare Reform: Five Key Realities," *Gallup Poll,* October 30, 2009, www.gallup.com/poll/123989/Americans-Healthcare-Reform-Five-Key-Realities.aspx.

16. Jeffrey M. Jones, "Majority of Americans Still Not Backing Healthcare Bill," *Gallup Poll,* December 16, 2009, www.gallup.com/poll/124715/Majority-Americans-Not-Backing-Healthcare-Bill.aspx.

17. Jeffrey M. Jones, "In U.S., Majority Favors Suspending Work on Healthcare Bill," *Gallup Poll*, January 22, 2010, www.gallup.com/poll/125327/Majority-Favors-Suspending-Work-Healthcare-Bill.aspx.

18. Frank Newport, "Obama Retains More Trust Than Congress on Healthcare," *Gallup Poll*, March 5, 2010, www.gallup.com/poll/126338/Obama-Retains-Trust-Congress-Healthcare.aspx.; Jeffrey M. Jones, "In U.S., 45% Favor, 48% Oppose Obama Healthcare Plan," *Gallup Poll*, March 9, 2010, www.gallup.com/poll/126521/Favor-Oppose-Obama-Healthcare-Plan.aspx.

19. Lydia Saad, "By Slim Margin, Americans Support Healthcare Bill's Passage," *Gallup Poll*, March 23, 2010, www.gallup.com/poll/126929/Slim-Margin-Americans-Support-Healthcare-Bill-Passage.aspx. Jeffrey M. Jones, "In U.S., 46% Favor, 40% Oppose Repealing Healthcare Law," *Gallup Poll,* January 7, 2010. www.gallup.com/poll/145496/Favor-Oppose-Repealing-Healthcare-Law.aspx.

20. Vice President Biden and White House Chief of Staff Emanuel both urged the president in summer 2009 to go the incremental route, finding areas of agreement with the Republicans and postponing broad reform until there was greater political support for it. Cohn, "How They Did It," 14.

21. Cohn, "How They Did It," 24.

22. Eli Saslow, "For a Look Outside Presidential Bubble, Obama Reads 10 Personal Letters Each Day," *Washington Post*, March 31, 2010, www.washingtonpost.com/wp-dyn/content/article/2010/03/30/AR2010033004260_2.html?sid=ST2010033004292.

23. Bob Woodward, *Obama's Wars* (New York: Simon & Schuster, 2010), 110.

24. Michael Hastings, "The Stanley McChrystal Scoop That Changed History: Stanley McChrystal, Obama's Top Commander in Afghanistan, Has Seized Control of the War by Never Taking His Eye Off the Real Enemy: The Wimps in the White House," June 22, 2010, www.rollingstone.com/politics/news/17390/119236.

25. Alter, *The Promise*, 132–33.

26. Ibid., 373.

27. Woodward, *Obama's Wars*, 205.

28. Ibid., 182.

29. Peter Baker, "How Obama Came to Plan for 'Surge' in Afghanistan," *New York Times*, December 6, 2009, www.nytimes.com/2009/12/06/world/asia/06reconstruct.html.

30. Woodward reports that the president asked the vice president to be a contrarian. He wanted vigorous debate on what he considered to be issues of life or death. Woodward, *Obama's Wars*, 160.

31. Frank Newport, "In U.S., More Support for Increasing Troops in Afghanistan," *Gallup Poll*, November 25, 2009, www.gallup.com/poll/124490/In-U.S.-More-Support-Increasing-Troops-Afghanistan.aspx.

32. Woodward, *Obama's Wars*, 195, 280.
33. Ibid, 305.
34. Ibid., 315
35. Ibid., 376.
36. Alter, *The Promise*, 385.
37. Frank Newport, "Obama's Plan for Afghanistan Finds Bipartisan Support," *Gallup Poll*, December 3, 2009, www.gallup.com/poll/124562/Obama-Plan-Afghanistan-Finds-Bipartisan-Support.aspx.
38. "Topics A–Z: Afghanistan," *Gallup Poll*, www.gallup.com/poll/116233/Afghanistan.aspx.
39. Scott Wilson and Michael D. Shear, "McChrystal Ousted from Afghan Post," *Washington Post*, June 24, 2010, A8, www.washingtonpost.com/wp-dyn/content/article/2010/06/23/AR2010062300689.html.
40. Barack Obama, "Statement by the President in the Rose Garden," June 23, 2010, www.whitehouse.gov/the-press-office/statement-president-rose-garden.

BIBLIOGRAPHY

Achenbach, Joel. "In His Slow Decision-Making, Obama Goes with Head, Not Gut." *Washington Post*, November 25, 2009. www.washingtonpost.com/wp-dyn/content/article/2009/11/24/AR2009112404225.html?hpid=topnews.

Adair, Bill, and Angie Drobnic Holan. "Rating Obama's Promises at the 1-Year Mark." PolitiFact.com, January 14, 2010. www.politifact.com/truth-o-meter/article/2010/jan/14/rating-obamas-promises-1-year-mark/.

Alter, Jonathan. *The Promise*. New York: Simon & Schuster, 2010.

Baker, Peter. "How Obama Came to Plan for 'Surge' in Afghanistan." *New York Times*, December 6, 2009. www.nytimes.com/2009/12/06/world/asia/06reconstruct.html.

Barber, James David. *The Presidential Character*. Englewood Cliffs, NJ: Prentice Hall, 1972.

Brody, David. "Obama to CBN News: We're No Longer Just a Christian Nation." *Christian Broadcast Network* (July 2007). www.cbn.com/CBNnews/204016.aspx.

Cohn, Jonathan. "How They did It," *New Republic* (June 10, 2010): 14–25.

Connolly, Ceci. "How Obama Revived His Health Care Bill." *Washington Post*, March 23, 2010. www.washingtonpost.com/wp-dyn/content/article/2010/03/22/AR2010032203729.html?hpid=topnews.

Enda, Jodi. "Great Expectations." *American Prospect*, January 16, 2006. www.prospect.org/cs/articles?articleId=10828.

Fox News. "Transcript: Obama on 'FNS.'" (April 27, 2008). http://elections.foxnews.com/2008/04/27/transcript-obama-on-fns.

Gold, Matea. "Jackson Apologizes for Crude Remark About Obama." *Los Angeles Times*, July 10, 2008. www.seattletimes.nwsource.com/html/nationworld/2008043111_campobama10.html.

Goldberg, Jeffrey. "Obama on Zionism and Hamas." *TheAtlantic.com*, (May 12, 2008. www.theatlantic.com/international/archive/2008/05/obama-on-zionism-and-hamas/8318.

Greenstein, Fred I. *The Presidential Difference*. New York: Free Press, 2000.

Holan, Angie Drobnic, Erin Mershon, and Lukas Pleva. "Checking Up on Obama's Campaign Promises." PolitiFact.com, June 25, 2010. http://www.politifact.com/truth-o-meter/article/2010/jun/25/checking-obamas-campaign-promises.

Jacobson, Louis. "Tracking Obama's Promises: One Step Forward, One Back," PolitiFact.com, November 12, 2010. www.politifact.com/truth-o-meter/article/2010/nov/29/tracking-obamas-promises-one-step-forward-one-back.

Kantor, Jodi. "Teaching Law, Testing Ideas, Obama Stood Slightly Apart." *New York Times,* July 30, 2008. www.nytimes.com/2008/07/30/us/politics/301aw.html.

King, Neil, Jr., and Jonathan Weisman. "A President as Micromanager: How Much Detail Is Enough?" *Wall Street Journal,* August 12, 2009. http://online.wsj.com/article/SB125003045380123953.html.

Klein, Joe. "The Full Obama Interview," *Time,* October 23, 2008. http://swampland.blogs.time.com/2008/10/23/the_full_obama_interview.

Kloppenberg, James T. *Reading Obama; Dreams, Hope, and the American Political Tradition.* Princeton, NJ: Princeton University Press, 2010.

Kornblut, Anne, Scott Wilson, and Karen DeYoung. "Obama Pressed for Faster Surge." *Washington Post,* December 5, 2009. www.washingtonpost.com/wp-dyn/content/article/2009/12/05/AR2009120501376.html.

Kroft, Steve. "Interview of Barack Obama on *"60 Minutes."* CBS News September 17, 2008. www.cbsnews.com/stories/2008/09/24/60minutes/main4476095.shtml.

———. "Interview of Barack Obama on *"60 Minutes."* CBS News March 20, 2009. www.cbsnews.com/stories/2009/03/24/60minutes/main4890684.shtml.

Leno, Jay. "Transcript of Obama Interview on *The Tonight Show.*" NBC March 20, 2009. http://online.wsj.com/article/SB123752189482892841.html.

Leonhardt, David. "After the Great Recession." *New York Times Magazine,* April 28, 2009, www.nytimes.com/2009/05/03/magazine/03Obama-t.html.

Lizza, Ryan. "Inside the Crisis: Larry Summers and the White House Economic Team." *The New Yorker,* October 12, 2009, www.newyorker.com/reporting/2009/10/12/091012fa_fact_lizza#ixzz0tVIkhe15.

———. "Making It." *The New Yorker,* July 21, 2008, 48–65. www.newyorker.com/reporting/2008/07/21/080721fa_fact_lizza.

MacFarquhar, Larissa. "The Conciliator." *The New Yorker,* May 7, 2007, 46–57.

Mark, David. "Obama Interview." *Politico* February 12, 2008. www.politico.com/news/stories/0208/8457_Page2.html.

Meacham, Jon. "Transcript of Obama Interview." *Newsweek,* September 1, 2008, 32.

Merida, Kevin. "How He Got Here: The Ghost of a Father." *Washington Post,* December 14, 2007, A13. Nagourney, Adam, and Jeff Zeleny. "Obama Forgoes Public Funds in First for Major Candidate." *New York Times,* June 20, 2008. www.washingtonpost.com/wp-dyn/content/story/2007/12/13/ST2007121301893.html.

New York Times. "Interview with Barack Obama" November 1, 2007. www.nytimes.com/2007/11/01/us/politics/02obama-transcript.html.

Obama, Barack. *The Audacity of Hope*. New York: Crown Publishers, 2006.
——. *Dreams from My Father*. New York: Three Rivers Press, 1995.
——. "Inaugural Address" January 20, 2009. www.whitehouse.gov.
——. "Interview on *the Daily Show* with Jon Stewart" October 27, 2010. www
.whitehouse.gov/blog/2010/10/27/president-obama-daily-show-with-jon-
stewart.
——. "Interview with NPR" June 1, 2009. www.npr.org/templates/story/story
.php?storyId=104806528.
——. "Keynote Address at the 2004 Democratic National Convention" July
27, 2004. www.barackobama.com/2004/07/27/keynote_address_at_the_
2004_de.php.
——. "Remarks by the President in a Youth Town Hall" October 14, 2010,
www.whitehouse.gov/the-press-office/2010/10/14/remarks-president-a-
youth-town-hall.
——. "Speech on Racial Relations" March 18, 2008. blogs.wsj.com/wash
wire/2008/03/18/text-of-obamas-speech-a-more-perfect-union.
"Obama's Media Image—Compared to What?" Center for Media and Public
Affairs, Press Release, January 25, 2010. www.cmpa.com/media_room_
press_1_25_10.html.
Plouffe, David. *The Audacity to Win*. New York: Viking, 2009.
Pulliam, Sarah, and Ted Olsen. "Q & A: Barack Obama," *Christianity Today*, June 2,
2008. www.ctlibrary.com/ct/2008/januaryweb-only/104-32.0.html.
Purdum, Todd. "Raising Obama." *Vanity Fair*, March 2008. www.vanityfair
.com/politics/features/2008/03/obama200803.
Remnick, David. *The Bridge: The Life and Rise of Barack Obama*. New York: Alfred
A. Knopf, 2010. www.newyorker.com/archive/2006/10/30/061030on_on
lineonly04.
——. "Testing the Waters." *The New Yorker*, October 30, 2006. www.newyorker
.com/archive/2006/10/30/0610300n_online.
Renshon, Stanley A. *The Psychological Assessment of Presidential Candidates*. New
York: Routledge, 1998.
Saslow, Eli. "A Rising Political Star Adopts a Low-Key Strategy." *Washington
Post*, October 17, 2008, A1, A6, A7.
Scott, Janny. "The Story of Obama, Written by Obama." *New York Times*, May 18,
2008. www.nytimes.com/2008/05/18/us/politics/18memoirs.html.
Sector, Bob, and John McCormick. "Barack Obama: Portrait of a Pragmatist."
Chicago Tribune, March 30, 2007, www.chicagotribune.com/news/nation
world/chi-0703300121mar30-archive,0,5213128.story.
Stephanopolous, George. "Transcript of Obama Interview." *ABC This Week*
January 11, 2009. abcnews.go.com/ThisWeek/Economy/story?id=6618199
&page=2.
Stolberg, Sheryl Gay, Jeff Zeleny, and Carl Hulse. "Health Vote Caps a Jour-
ney Back from the Brink." *New York Times*, March 20, 2010, www.nytimes
.com/2010/03/21/health/policy/21reconstruct.html.
Thai, Xuan, and Ted Barrett. "Biden's Description of Obama Draws Scrutiny."
CNN February 9, 2007. www.associatedcontent.com/article/978364/barack_
obama_introduces_joe_biden_pg2.html.

Walsh, Kenneth T. "David Axelrod. Auto-Bailout, Torture Memos Among Obama's Toughest Decisions." *U.S. News & World Report*, June 10, 2009. www.politics.usnews.com/news/articles/2009/03/11/david-axelrod-auto-bailout-torture-memos.

———. "Obama Defends Waiting on Afghanistan Decision." *U.S. News & World Report*, October 27, 2009. www.usnews.com/.../articles/2009/10/27/obama-defends-waiting-on-afghanistan-decision.html.

Warner, Margaret. "Confidence, Openness Mark Obama's Decision Making Style." *News Hour* September 23, 2008, www.pbs.org/newshour/bb/politics/july-dec08/obamacloseup_09-23.html.

Wenner, Jann S. "A Conversation with Barack Obama." *Rolling Stone*, July 10, 2008. www.jannswenner.com/Archives/Barack_Obama.aspx.

———. "Obama in Command: The *Rolling Stone* Interview" (October 15, 2010). www.rollingstone.com/politics/news/17390/209395.

"White House Watch: Obama's First Year." *Media Monitor* 24 (Quarter 1, 2010). www.cmpa.com/pdf/media_monitor_q1_2010.pdf.

Woodward, Bob. *Obama's Wars*. New York: Simon & Schuster, 2010.

Zeleny, Jeff. "Obama Adding Detail to His Oratory." *New York Times*, February 17, 2008. www.nytimes.com/2008/02/17/us/politics/17obama.html.

Zeleny, Jeff, and Jim Rutenberg. "A Delegator, Obama Picks When to Take Reins." *New York Times*, June 16, 2008. www.nytimes.com/2008/06/16/us/politics/16manage.html.

INDEX

*Boxes, figures, notes, and tables are indicated by
b, f, n, and t following page numbers.*

Pharmaceutical industry, deal with,
121, 132
Plouffe, David, 55, 58, 74, 112
Polarized political system, 88–89,
97–99
Policy czars, 59
Politics of consensus, 39–40
PolitiFact.com, 117
Popularity, 83–84
Pragmatism, 44–46, 54, 73–74
President-elect, Obama as, 31, 91,
127–128
Presidential campaign (2008)
anger, displays of, 62
enlarging Democratic Party base,
112, 119, 124n28
federal funding, pledge to take, 20
McCain's inconsistent behavior as
issue, 6, 12n13
media, distance from, 61
Obama vs. Clinton, 24, 81
organization behind Obama, 58, 74
promises and policy challenges, 81,
88, 104, 117–118
racial characterization of Obama
during, 14, 27n2
The Presidential Character (Barber), 5
Presidential Power (Neustadt), 4
Presidential power, limits of, 97–102
constitutional framework, 97
institutional rivalry, 99–102
polarized political system, 97–99
Problem solving, 74–75
Progressive pragmatism, 44–46
Project for Excellence in Journalism,
123n16
Promises during campaign. *See*
Presidential campaign (2008)
Public opinion, 133–137
conservatives vs. moderates vs.
liberals, 107n19
on government, 65, 102–104,
103–104t
Obama's inability to change, 110,
122, 129
prior to reelection, 119
at time of 2008 election, 119

Qualitative studies, 4
Quantitative studies, 4

Race and roots, 14–18, 26, 27n2
Race relations speech (2008
campaign), 31, 39, 53, 63, 81
Racism, 39
Rationality vs. empathy, 52, 77–81
Rattner, Steven, 75
Reagan, Nancy, 61, 68n23
Reagan, Ronald
ease in Washington, 1
empathy of, 80
ideological views of, 7
Obama's difference from, 40
Obama's similarities with, 33, 47n3,
60, 64
Recession, 115
Recovery and Reinvestment Act, 92, 105
Redistribution of wealth to address
inequality, 41, 49n43
Regulation and role of government,
40–42, 49n42
Reid, Harry, 21, 22, 134
Relatedness, 7
Religion, 35–37
Remnick, David, 18, 22, 28–29n22, 62
Renshon, Stanley, 5, 7
Repression of emotions. *See* Emotions,
display of
Republican opposition to Obama
Afghanistan policy, 139
bailouts, 98, 106n6
health care reform, 98, 101, 133,
137
immigration issue, 107n8
job approval rating of Obama, 99,
99f
slowing down legislation, 92
Republicans, Obama's willingness to
work with, 76–77, 135. *See also*
Bipartisanship
Republican support of Afghanistan
policy, 107n10
Roll call votes, 4, 11n3
Rolling Stone article with McChrystal,
141–142